ALLEG HF5549.5.T7 M536 1989
Miller, Kathleen D.
Retraining the American workforce

3036000000058186

HF 5549.5 .T7 M536 1989
Miller, Kathleen D.
Retraining the American
workforce

DATE DUE

THE COMMUNITY COLLEGE OF ALLEGHENY COUNTY
ALLEGHENY CAMPUS
808 RIDGE AVENUE
PITTSBURGH, PA.
15212
LIBRARY

VOID

Retraining the American Workforce

Retraining the American Workforce

KATHLEEN D. MILLER

Addison-Wesley Publishing Company Inc.
Reading, Massachusetts   Menlo Park, California   New York
Don Mills, Ontario   Wokingham, England   Amsterdam
Bonn   Sydney   Singapore   Tokyo   Madrid   San Juan

Library of Congress Cataloging-in-Publication Data
Miller, Kathleen D.
　　Retraining the American workforce / Kathleen D. Miller.
　　p.　cm.
　　Includes index.
　　ISBN 0-201-11585-9
　　1. Employees, Training of—United States.　2. Career changes—
United States.　3. Occupational retraining—United States.
4. Corporate planning—United States.　　I. Title.
HF5549.5.T7M536　1989　　658.3' 1243—dc19　　　88-7505

Tables 3–1, 3–2, 3–3, and 3–4 are reprinted with permission from the October 1987 issue of *TRAINING, The Magazine of Human Resources Development.* Copyright © 1987, Lakewood Publications Inc., Minneapolis, MN (612) 333-0471. All rights reserved.

Copyright © 1989 by Kathleen D. Miller. All rights reserved. No part of this publication may be reproduced, stored in a retrieval system, or transmitted, in any form or by any means, electronic, mechanical, photocopying, recording, or otherwise, without the prior written permission of the publisher. Printed in the United States of America. Published simultaneously in Canada.

Editor: Scott Shershow
Production Coordinator: Lynne Reed
Cover design by Mike Fender
Text design by Joyce C. Weston
Set in 10 point Trump by DEKR Corp., Woburn, MA

ISBN 0-201-11585-9
ABCDEFGHIJ-DO-89
First printing, January 1989

Contents

Preface ix
Acknowledgments xi

1. Retraining: The Urgent Challenge for Corporate America 1

What Is Retraining? 5
Who Is Responsible for Retraining? 7
Who Gets Involved within a Company? 7
References 8

2. The Changing Workplace: Restructuring, Reevaluating, and Retooling 9

Displaced Workers: Who and How Many? 9
Restructuring the Economy 11
Adjusting to Technology 15
Technology Affects Skills Requirements 17
Job Design and Skills Requirements 18
Technical Skills 22
Technology Affects the Nature of Work 24
Changing Skills for Managers 25
The Role of Corporate Culture 28
Summary and Implications 30
References 32

3. Sharing the Challenge: Partnerships for Retraining 34

Overview of Workplace Training 34
Remedial Education 35
Occupational Retraining 43
Partnerships for Retraining 43
Summary and Implications 51
References 52

Contents

4. Developing a Strategic Plan: Linking Retraining to Corporate Goals 54

Why Link Training to Long-Range Strategic Plans? 54
Soliciting Input from the Top 55
Distinguishing Long-Term from Short-Term Personnel Plans 56
Assessing Demand: Projecting Skill Requirements 59
Assessing Supply: Identifying Employees' Skills 61
Checking for Imbalances 63
Cost/Benefit Comparisons 64
Summary and Implications 67
References 67

5. Planning and Administering the Program: Who Does What and When? 68

Forming the Retraining Program Team 68
Developing the Program Plan 73
Developing the Curriculum Plan 83
Announcing and Publicizing the Program 89
Implementation 92
Evaluation 94
Special Issues 96
Summary and Implications 97
References 98

6. Facilitating Transition: Smooth Endings and New Beginnings 99

Keeping Up with Change: Career Planning 99
Preparing the Company for Change 107
Facilitating the Retrainees' Transitions 110
Summary and Implications 119
References 121

7. Retraining the Older Worker: Different Requirements? 122

Why Retrain Older Workers? 122
Who Are Older Workers? 125

Contents

Characteristics of Older Workers   128
Intellectual Performance and Age   129
Getting Older Workers into Retraining Programs   131
Older Learners in the Classroom   133
Summary and Implications   141
References   143

8. Summary and Conclusions   144

Basic Skill Deficiencies Block Retraining   145
Employers Vary in Their Commitment to Training   146
Training and Long-Range Planning: The Strategic Link   148
Successful Retraining Requires Careful Planning   149
Keeping Up with Change   151
Retraining Can Be Stressful   152
It Is Never Too Late to Retrain   152
Conclusions   153
References   154

Index   155

Preface

POWERFUL economic, technological, and societal trends are transforming work in America. As nearly half of the jobs in the U.S. economy are transformed or replaced every five to eight years, American workers face the need to repeatedly acquire new skills over their work lives. A company's ability to remain competitive and thus to survive dramatic market changes depends on employees who possess the skills to perform their jobs. By retraining the workforce American companies not only can hold their ground but can thrive in the changing global economy.

Purpose and Audience

Companies must respond to the urgent need for private-sector involvement in retraining the workforce. This book promotes awareness of the problem and also outlines specific steps that corporations can follow to establish retraining programs.

I wrote the book for the executives, corporate planners, and personnel and human resource development managers and staff within companies who make decisions that affect skill requirements. Others involved in corporate education and training should find this material useful, as will communications managers, whose departments play a key role in establishing a climate that facilitates the retraining process. Although this book was not written primarily as a textbook, the information presented here is useful to students preparing for corporate careers.

What Makes This Book Unique

This book differs from other publications that examine retraining by its focus on the private sector rather than the public sector. Until recently, retraining has been viewed primarily as the responsibility of federal and state governments. This book, however, concentrates on how leaders of corporations can keep their employees abreast of changes. It outlines proactive approaches designed to prevent large-scale deficiencies and dislocation within all areas of the workforce.

Preface

Organization of Chapters

The first three chapters of the book examine the context for addressing private-sector involvement in retraining. Chapter 1 addresses the scope of the skill obsolescence and personnel shortage problems, and Chapter 2 looks at the forces that are changing skill requirements. Chapter 3 describes the magnitude and nature of the private-sector training enterprise. It also gives an overview of various cooperative efforts that have been organized to provide retraining programs, such as public-private partnerships as well as union-management team projects.

Chapters 4 and 5 explore the mechanics of identifying the need for retraining and planning and administering the programs. These chapters are written from the "how to" point of view. Chapter 5 offers an especially detailed discussion of how to put together a program from beginning to end.

Chapter 6 emphasizes the very human and personal side of the retraining experience. It is based on the experiences and comments of trainees with whom I have worked over the past ten years and recommends approaches for facilitating career changes throughout a company and for assisting trainees with the inevitable stress that accompanies transitions.

Chapter 7 presents an overview of research on the characteristics and requirements of older learners and explains why it is crucial to include older adults in the retraining process.

Chapter 8 summarizes the importance of retraining, key ways to address the retraining process and, finally, draws conclusions about who is responsible for meeting this challenge of the future.

Acknowledgments

This book is the result of ten years of experience in working with retraining programs. I would like to express my gratitude to all of those courageous adults who have participated in the retraining process. I am grateful for their willingness to share their concerns as well as their triumphs with me.

I would also like to thank Denice Weber, Roger Sugarman, and Vicki Dennis for their assistance in editing. Thanks go to Sandra Skinner for assisting with the typing.

Special acknowledgment is due my secretary, Cecilia Stephens, not only for helping with the research and typing the manuscript but also for taking more than her share of the responsibilities for operating the office while I wrote the book.

I am especially indebted to Jackie Cheaturn, a colleague with whom I collaborated on the development and implementation of many of the programs described in this book. Her comments and ideas stimulated me to develop many of the strategies which I recommended in these pages.

Finally, special thanks to David Richart, whose sense of humor, valuable insight, and constant encouragement helped me complete this project.

CHAPTER ONE

♦

Retraining: *The Urgent Challenge for Corporate America*

A TOOL AND DIE MAKER working in the automotive industry is training to become a specialist in the computer-aided design and manufacturing of parts. He must make the transition from working with paper drawings and manually machining parts on the factory floor to sitting in front of a computer terminal in a quiet office and manipulating coordinates on the screen.

A middle manager who has worked for fifteen years in a food-processing facility has been told that workers on the plant floor must have more autonomy and greater input into the decision-making process. The manager must acquire the skills to move from a directive, controlling management style to a participative, facilitative style. Moreover, the manager must learn to use a computer and must develop an understanding of data-based management in order to survive in the new business environment.

An assembler who has worked on the line in a typewriter manufacturing facility for twenty years has learned that her job will soon be automated. She must return to the classroom for the first time in twenty years to retrain for a new occupation or face unemployment.

In my work within corporate America over the last few years, I have seen workers at every level face the challenge of mastering sweeping changes in the skills required to perform productively in the workplace. Companies of all sizes and types have been affected by new technologies, fluctuating international markets, deregulation, and shifts from a manufacturing-based to an information-based economy. I have assisted corporate planners, personnel departments, and technical trainers in their search for solutions to the skill obsolescence predicament. I also have worked with several thousand people who were involved in various aspects of corporate retraining and assisted in the planning, design, and delivery of programs ranging from computer programming to robot maintenance. It was through grappling with the issues and realities of retraining, that I became aware of the magnitude and severity of the problem. This book emerged from these experiences.

By the year 2000, between 5 to 15 million manufacturing jobs will be restructured, approximately the same number of service jobs will become obsolete, and an estimated 16 million new jobs will be created. In general, the new jobs will require higher levels of skills than did the jobs that become obsolete. Not only will the mix of available jobs change, but the very nature of work will be altered to suit the new technologies. Thus, American businesses are faced with a potential mismatch between the skills that will be available in the workforce and the skills that will be required for the workplace. This mismatch is likely to create hardships for workers in the form of job displacement and cause problems for companies in the form of personnel shortages.

Our nation's attention has belatedly turned to one side of the skill mismatch dilemma. Economists, labor leaders, and politicians have directed much concern to the serious problem of displaced workers—people who are unemployed and unlikely to return to their previous occupations because their skills have become obsolete. A recent study conducted by the Congressional Office of Technology Assessment reported that 5.1 million American workers were displaced between 1979 and 1984 because of some permanent structural changes in the economy. Indeed, estimates of the number of people who face displacement over the next decade range from 10 to 15 million. Industrial robots alone are predicted to displace 200,000 blue-collar workers by 1990 (Hunt and Hunt 1983).

Blue-collar workers are not unique in facing the effect of skill shifts. White-collar workers, including managers, also are displaced as offices automate and organizations decentralize. In fact, between 1981 and 1983 half of the *Fortune* 1300 companies eliminated an entire layer of management primarily because new, decentralized organizational structures have been made possible by electronic information management systems (Snyder 1984). Close to a half million managers have left their companies since 1984, some voluntarily, but many others as a consequence of company cutbacks. "The critical question for a lot of middle managers," observes Robert Smith, director of human resources at the Battelle Memorial Institute, "is whether their skills are ever going to be needed again. The answer is no—unless they are willing to start over" ("Who Will Retrain the Obsolete Managers?" 1983: 80).

In addition to the familiar problems of increased foreign competition and a volatile world economy, perhaps the greatest single cause of displacement is the rapid technological innovation of business, and the rate of displacement is likely to increase as the pace of this innovation accelerates. Some experts forecast that our country could experience as much workforce displacement in the next twenty years as it has seen in the past eighty years (National Alliance of Business 1986).

Although much recent attention has been focused on the displacement dilemma, far less attention has been directed toward the potential worker shortages that could result from the skill mismatch. Employers can no longer rely on filling newly created jobs solely through new hires because the number of youths entering the workforce has decreased and will continue to drop. Roughly 75 percent of those who will be part of the workforce in the year 2000 are already working (National Alliance of Business 1986). Moreover, the qualifications of those persons who *will* enter the workforce are declining as the numbers of high school dropouts and functionally illiterate adults surge. The U.S. Department of Education and the National Science Foundation have reported that the United States is becoming virtually illiterate in science and technology (Naisbitt 1982). Widespread deficiencies in science and math could mean that workforce entrants will not have the qualifications to perform the jobs created by sophisticated technologies in the year 2000.

Indeed, our country is already experiencing a shortage of workers with critical technical skills. Even though the average age of our nation's skilled machinists is fifty-eight, we are training only one-fourth of the machinists needed each year (National Alliance of Business 1986). This trend toward fewer and less qualified entrants into the workforce, coupled with the upward shift in skill requirements, could prove to be disastrous for companies that do not take immediate steps to avoid a worker crisis.

The skill mismatch problem that affects job displacement, as well as worker shortages, is complex and requires innovative solutions. Certainly private-sector retraining is not a panacea. Some critics have pointed out that these programs face stumbling blocks such as the lack of basic learning skills in a portion of the workforce and labor unions that may resist retraining because many retrained workers move out of union jobs. In my experience, however, most labor unions favor retraining as contributing to job security. My work with successful programs over the last few years has convinced me that well-planned retraining can begin to address the skill mismatch crisis.

Retraining is no longer simply a public-sector responsibility. In fact, just as the workforce is beginning to be affected by major technological changes, the federal government is reducing spending. Retraining activities under the Job Training Partnership Act, for example, have been cut by 50 percent and currently serve only a fraction of displaced workers. Moreover, data comparing the effectiveness of various retraining options indicate that the most productive and cost-efficient programs are those that prepare employees to fill jobs with the same employer (Snyder 1984). Thus, the private sector must address the retraining challenge if worker shortages, as well as the overwhelming hardships of displaced workers, are to be avoided.

While the private sector faces a skill mismatch problem that demands immediate action, executives in major corporations often fail to place a high priority on human resource planning. A 1984 Opinion Research Corporation survey of top executives at large corporations found that executives viewed becoming more productive and more competitive as high priorities but looked on long-term workforce planning and retraining workers to use new technologies as considerably less significant concerns (Fisher 1986). Corporate heads apparently fail to make the vital connection between productivity and human resource planning and training and to recognize that a company's survival depends on the availability of workers equipped with suitable skills.

What Is Retraining?

The key to maintaining a productive workforce with the appropriate skill mix is to tie training and retraining programs to strategic and long-range planning. Top-level executives must provide information concerning the company's overall strategic mission and future direction if training and retraining programs are to be built on real business needs rather than on the latest fads within the human resource development community. By linking human resource planning to strategic business planning, companies can take a preventative approach to the skill mismatch challenge. Instead of waiting to react after a skill mix crisis has occurred, companies can retrain employees to match projected skill needs.

What Is Retraining?

Throughout the 1980s the term *retraining* has appeared frequently in the popular media and repeatedly in recently negotiated labor contracts. For example, in one of the most recent GM-UAW labor agreements, GM promised to spend as much as $1 billion over six years to retrain, transfer, or otherwise support workers threatened by automation. Likewise, the job security provision of the 1986 settlement between AT&T and the Communications Workers of America rests heavily on the establishment of retraining programs (Pollock 1986). In fact, most policies of employment security move employees out of jobs that are being phased out and into high-demand jobs. Retraining is an essential step in that process (Rosow 1987).

The word *retraining* can be heard in corporate boardrooms and in congressional hearings. Indeed, around 1983 the issue of retraining became a top priority of our nation's leaders. Terms such as *high-technology training*, *retraining*, and *training for displaced workers* became key phrases in the Ninety-eighth Congress. In spite of such widespread usage, however, the word lacks a clear and consistent definition.

How *Retraining* Differs from *Training*

As used in this book, *retraining* refers to training that leads a worker to a significantly different job or career. A person who previously worked as an assembler in a factory must retrain to make the transition into computer programming. The old role is radically different from the new role, and the transition requires extensive training in technical skills as well as adjusting to a very different working environment. The assembler moves from the plant floor to an office and from blue-collar work to a white-collar profession.

Often retraining is associated with a total change of career, but sometimes the skills required to perform a job change so radically that individuals must retrain even though they may remain within the same career. The term *retraining* could apply to programs for preparing traditional quality inspectors to undertake statistical methods of quality control. Under the old process, the inspector's role involved identifying and discarding work that did not meet specifications. The new role requires identifying the variable in the production process that accounts for the defects in the product. The nature of an inspector's role changes with the statistical method, and inspectors usually must return to the classroom for extensive course work covering such topics as experimental design, statistics, and engineering economics. Not only does the new role require the acquisition of technical knowledge, but it also requires a new cooperative relationship between the quality engineer and other people involved in the production process. The quality inspector becomes a problem-solver rather than a watchdog. Certainly such major changes fall within the definition of *retraining* in spite of the lack of change in career path.

Compared to *training* programs, *retraining* programs are aimed at helping employees make major transitions. Employees are required not only to learn new skills but to be resocialized. New attitudes, values, and assumptions are required about the relationship between the individual and work. Because these transitions generally encompass much more than the simple acquisition of a new skill or method for performing a job, retraining programs are unique. Retraining is often more stressful than regular training and program planners need to be sensitive to the exceptional pressures that accompany the process. Unlike more limited skill training, retraining affects many aspects of the trainees' work roles and, indeed, their whole lives. Trainers and managers concerned with retraining programs must find a way to help trainees cope with these changes.

Who Is Responsible for Retraining?

Retraining our labor force is so great a task that no one sector of the economy can shoulder the entire burden. The challenge must be shared by both the public and private sectors. Although federal, state, and local governments are likely to continue to take primary responsibility for retraining disadvantaged groups and the hard-core unemployed, companies within the private sector must provide retraining opportunities for their own employees. Companies benefit from the retraining that they offer employees in a number of ways. The retraining establishes a stable, loyal workforce. The company becomes less vulnerable to worker shortages and it eliminates the time and money involved in recruiting new employees. When the company retrains its existing employees, training can build on the knowledge and experience that trainees have accumulated over their years with the company. As Jerome Rosow from the Work in America Institute summarizes (Rosow 1987),

> Investment in learning strengthens the competitiveness of an employer and increases its ability to provide employment security. Educated employees are capable of a surprising amount of adaptation to the changing needs of the enterprise.

Who Gets Involved within a Company?

Retraining programs require the coordinated involvement of several departments within a company, including the education and training department. For example, because the programs often involve career change and sometimes relocation, personnel departments help with the selection and placement of trainees. Likewise, communications departments generally participate in the retraining process by handling internal and external publicity. Retraining programs commonly receive attention from people throughout the company and even throughout the community. Employees are frequently concerned with issues such as who will be retrained and what will happen to people who are not retrained. If the company has a strong presence in a community, local leaders and citizens are interested in the business conditions that led to the retraining and in the company's employment plans for the immediate future.

The dissemination of information about these issues should be handled by experienced professionals.

Frequently programs need not only the active participation of several departments within the company but also outside providers such as educational institutions and consultants. Companies may turn to outside experts for assistance with the skills analyses and projections on which retraining programs are built. Furthermore, companies may not have the internal resources to deliver the variety of courses and training experiences required for certain programs. Whether the company uses internal or external sources of training, all those involved with the delivery of the programs must be aware of the special needs of the trainees who face the pressures of major career transition.

References

Fisher, J. A. 1986. "Forging a Link between Technology and Training." *Personnel* (April).

Hunt, H. A., and Hunt, T. 1983. *Human Resource Implications of Robotics.* Kalamazoo, Mich.: W. E. Upjohn Institute for Employment Research.

Naisbitt, J. 1982. *Megatrends.* New York: Warren Books.

National Alliance of Business. 1986. *Employment Policies: Looking to the Year 2000.* Washington, D.C.: NAB Clearinghouse, February.

Pollock, M. A. 1986. "AT&T's Hard Bargain: A Watershed for the Industry?" *Business Week* (June 30).

Rosow, J. M., and Zager, R. 1987. *Training for New Technology Part II: The Continuous Learning/Employment Security Connection.* Scarsdale, N.Y.: Work in America Institute.

Snyder, D. P. 1984. *The Strategic Context of Management in America 1985 to 1995.* Bethesda, Md.: Snyder Family Enterprise.

"Who Will Retrain the Obsolete Managers?" 1983. *Business Week* (April 25).

CHAPTER TWO

◆

The Changing Workplace: *Restructuring, Reevaluating, and Retooling*

Economic, technological, and societal trends are accelerating to the point where nearly all American workers will be affected by major changes in the nature of their jobs before their work lives are over. Presently, with nearly half of the jobs in the U.S. economy transformed or replaced every five to eight years, workers must acquire new skills for new careers every few years throughout their entire work life. National attention has focused primarily on those who are most likely to lose their jobs as a result of structural changes in the economy, such as blue-collar workers employed in declining industries like heavy manufacturing. Although the severity of the crises of job losses cannot be overlooked, nearly all of us who work face the threat that our knowledge and skills are rapidly becoming obsolete. None of us can afford to become complacent.

Because the changing workplace is likely to affect all of us, we must examine the forces that drive those changes and the relationship between these changes and the structure of retraining programs. The pertinent issues include identifying who is facing displacement, how economic and technological changes affect skill requirements, and how these changes affect corporate cultures.

Displaced Workers: Who and How Many?

Although experts argue over the definition of who is displaced, all agree that displacement is a significant and long-term trend. The Office of Technology Assessment recently reported that between

1979 and 1985, 11.5 million American workers who had held jobs for three or more years lost their jobs because of plant closings or relocations, increased productivity, or foreign competition. Approximately half of these workers were in manufacturing (Office of Technology Assessment 1986). The hardest hit were typically white males in blue-collar manufacturing jobs in the Midwest or Northeast, but substantial numbers of women and minorities were also victims of these widespread job eliminations. Displaced workers on the whole had less education and lower levels of skills than more fortunate job retainers. Older workers, women, and minorities experienced the greatest difficulty in finding new jobs, and close to half of all the displaced workers who *did* find new jobs experienced pay cuts.

These current displacement figures are discouraging. Even more alarming are the future projections concerning job loss and displacement. By most estimates, 10 to 15 million manufacturing employees and an equal number of service workers are likely to face displacement within the next decade. The displacement dilemma will not affect only blue-collar workers. Indeed, everyone who performs manual labor or routine mental tasks in all sectors of the economy is vulnerable. The Office of Technology Assessment has predicted that by 1990 nearly every office will have at least one computer and that office productivity will increase significantly, but that employment levels in data entry and other clerical/support occupations are likely to be reduced. Likewise, fewer managers may be needed as computer technology increases the span of management control and as the tasks of lower-level managers are automated. Tasks currently performed by paraprofessionals and technical white-collar workers also will be automated. Some have suggested that the older, middle-class, white-collar, managerial and professional workers will be hit hardest by the next wave of unemployment, displacement, and general disruption (Perelman 1985).

Of course, the potential negative impact of automation on white-collar employment could be offset by growth in the volume of information handling. As new uses and needs for information are generated, the workload in offices may increase, so that the growth in demand for information could offset the reduction in labor associated with information handling. Nevertheless, the white-collar

Restructuring the Economy

workforce is going to be affected by displacement over the next decade. In fact, a substantial number of office workers have already become displaced: Between 1984 and 1986 an estimated 1 million white-collar employees left their companies due to cost-cutting staff reductions.

The current and future skill obsolescence problem is serious and widespread as millions of workers with outdated skills face the traumatic experience of job loss. Nearly all of us will face this dilemma at some point in our careers, but we can prevent a severe skill obsolescence crisis by formulating strategies now based on the economic and technological trends that point to future changes in skill requirements. (See Figure 2–1 for a summary of how a variety of forces affects skill requirements.)

Restructuring the Economy

The United States is presently experiencing a stunning shift in the relative dominance of economic sectors, and tracking this transition is crucial to developing effective retraining strategies. The various

**Figure 2–1
Organizational Factors Affecting Skill Requirements**

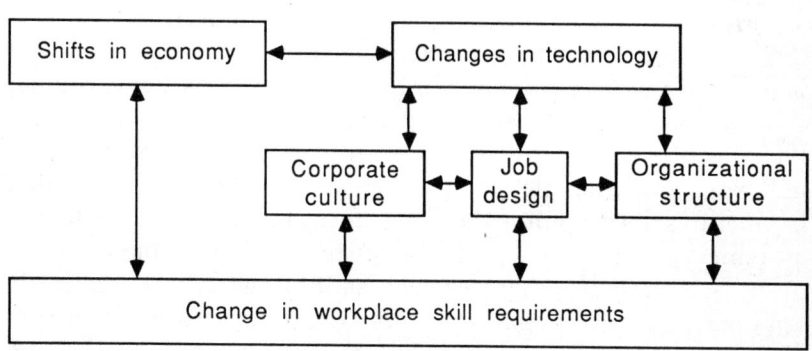

economic sectors contain different types of jobs that have divergent educational and skill requirements. Therefore, employment shifts among sectors can change the education and training that workers need to perform productively in the workplace (Rumberger 1986).

The major shift over the past two decades has been from the manufacturing sector to the service sector. Although manufacturing continues to be important to the economy, employment levels there fell by 900,000 jobs from 1980 to 1985. Over those years manufacturing's share of total employment dropped from 24 percent to 18 percent. At the same time, employment in the service sector showed tremendous growth. Service industries such as banking, real estate, finance, legal services, and health care currently account for over two-thirds of all American jobs (Choate and Linger 1986).

This unprecedented growth in services is likely to continue through the next decade. The Bureau of Labor Statistics forecasts the creation of 14 million service jobs between 1984 and 1995, compared to only 2 million new jobs in the goods-producing industries (Choate and Linger 1986). These figures mean that even though high technology manufacturing could absorb some displaced workers, many will simply lose their manufacturing jobs and seek reemployment in the service sector.

In addition to the changes in sector dominance, some changes within manufacturing are also leading to increases in service jobs. The mix of occupations within manufacturing industries is shifting to include more white-collar and service jobs. As the demand for unskilled assembly-line workers dwindles, the need for service technicians who can work on highly automated manufacturing systems increases (Choate and Linger 1986). Not only do manufacturers need more service workers to run their internal operations, but consumer demands have forced them to become more service oriented with their customers. This trend is especially prevalent in the high tech industries. For example, computer manufacturers are finding that in order to sell computers they must focus on helping the potential customers identify the specific ways in which the computer can meet their needs. Companies such as IBM and AT&T frequently send out application teams to work with their customers in conducting systems analyses. They help the customers assess the kind of hardware and software they need and often provide training and other installation assistance. Some companies, such as General Electric, will send internal consultants to work with customers' transition teams to oversee the installation of its products. Thus, not only will service *industries* account for a larger proportion of employment over the next decade, but service *occupations* will account for a larger percentage of jobs even within the manufacturing sector.

As the economy becomes increasingly service dominated, the skill and education requirements for the workplace will change. Unfortunately, because service jobs are so diverse, projecting the changing needs is difficult. Some service industries such as fast-foods, personal services, and nursing homes contain relatively low-skill and low-wage occupations. Other services such as insurance, wholesale trade, and auto repair represent occupations that are closer to the middle of the education and wage continuum. Finally, jobs in computers, legal services, and communications tend to fall at the higher end of this continuum. The server in a fast-food restaurant does not need the same level of basic skills as a legal aide or a computer technician.

In spite of this diversity, economists predict that the continued growth of the service sector will increase the level of skills and education required for participation in the workforce. The employment of high-level, white-collar professionals, technicians, and managerial-administrative personnel is much higher in the services overall than in manufacturing (Rumberger 1986), and the services already employ high-level manpower at twice the rate of the manufacturing. The most rapidly growing service job categories are in highly demanding information- or knowledge-based businesses such as financial, legal, and engineering services. Economist Eli Ginzberg summed up the connection between educational requirements and the predominance of the service industries when he stated that "the shift of the economy towards services is currently making it more difficult for the undereducated to find a niche. An increasingly white-collar economy has no place for functional illiterates" (Ginzberg 1985).

This expansion of service-sector and service occupations not only will raise the *level* of educational and skill needs but also will change the *nature* of these requirements. Service industries and occupations tend to be unique in that direct, personal contact often is made between the producer of the service and the consumer. Therefore, a service transaction in all types of companies and businesses frequently includes a social interaction. For example, a major part of a management consultant's job involves meeting with clients, discussing projects, and diagnosing problems. Likewise the successful performances of auto mechanics, retail clerks, and bank tellers depend on their abilities to interact with customers, understand their requests, and handle their complaints. As a result, interpersonal skills are generally critical for service occupations as diverse as waiting on tables and practicing law. Not only must service employees be capable of performing technical aspects of the job, they also must be able to communicate clearly, show tact, and demonstrate an understanding of the customers' needs (Mills 1986, p. 133).

Service occupations also differ from manufacturing occupations in the amount of freedom that the worker has in determining what to do and how to do it. Service employees generally have a great deal of discretion in setting their priorities and organizing their time. People who work on a traditional assembly line in factories usually have clearly prescribed roles. Their time is controlled by the parts that flow down the line and the specific directions of their supervisors. They begin their work and quit at the same time every day, and they have designated break times. On the other hand, secretaries rarely have their time rigidly organized for them. They may be expected to perform a variety of tasks for several people and may or may not be given directions concerning the relative importance and time frame for each task. In some cases, they may have designated break times, while in other cases, they are expected to fit their breaks into their schedule as the work permits. Of course, the degree to which employees have discretionary time will vary with different occupations. Certainly the check-out person in a grocery store does not have as much freedom as the salesperson calling on clients.

Because service occupations overall place more responsibility for organizing time on the employee than do manufacturing occupations, the shift toward a service economy and the expansion of service jobs raises the educational, technical, interpersonal, and self-management skill requirements for the workforce.

Adjusting to Technology

A second major force exerting an influence on skill requirements is the rapidly changing state of technology. Indeed, close to half of us working in the United States have already experienced major technological changes in our jobs (Choate and Linger 1986). The effect of technology on the workplace and workforce has been enormous over the last decade, and no end to technological innovation is in sight. Microprocessor technology is persistently and pervasively influencing the occupational and skill mix within the workplace. It is impossible to predict precisely how technology will affect occupations in the future, but some consequences are clear. Unskilled personnel such as auto workers or coal miners will not grow in numbers because new technologies have led to productivity gains with fewer workers in these industries. In the automotive industry, for example, low-skill jobs such as painting and welding are being automated as are some semiskilled jobs such as machine operations and inspections. In fact, some higher-skill production jobs such as machinists and tool and die makers are also being eliminated.

Automation has not touched only manufacturing operations. Occupations in service industries have also felt the effects of the computer. For example, automatic teller machines in the banking industry have replaced human bank tellers. Likewise, within the telephone service industry, computerized switching and direct long-distance dialing have increased productivity and decreased needs for telephone operators. On the other hand, demand for professional and semiprofessional jobs as well as sales, construction, installation, and maintenance jobs has grown (Office of Technology Assessment 1986).

In general, microprocessor technology has decreased the need for production workers in factories and for data entry and transfer clerical workers in offices. However, computers have led to the need for more computer progammers, analysts, network personnel, microcomputer specialists, artificial intelligence experts, and electrical and mechanical engineers.

The effect of automation has not been restricted to hourly employees. In fact, one major occupational effect of technology is the elimination of large numbers of lower and middle managers. Advances in computer and communications technologies have already brought about cuts of entire layers of managers. Between 1981 and 1983 over half of the *Fortune* 1300 companies abolished at least one layer of management, and this "delayering" of management is likely to continue (Snyder 1984). Some forecasters predict that 3 to 5 million middle managers will lose their jobs within the next decade.

Consistent with this trend, the corporate structure that is emerging as most functional for the computer age is flatter than the traditional pyramid. Historically, the organizational pyramid has been an efficient structure for the transmission of information from top to bottom in a company. Middle managers collected data from the rank and file and relayed it upward to those in top management positions. These upper-level managers would then make decisions, in part because they were the only individuals who had access to the overall picture. The decision would then be communicated back down through the layers of middle managers. This system of transmitting information is no longer the most efficient in the present business environment. Today, business and operating conditions fluctuate frequently and require quick responses. For instance, in highly automated factories, production "up time" requirements are very high at the same time that management and design conditions are constantly fluctuating. If disaster is to be avoided, potential problems must be rapidly detected and corrected. The traditional pyramid does not permit quick decision making. These rapid responses require the people who are closest to the problems to take more responsibility for prevention and correction. Moreover, the people at the top of the pyramid no longer have *exclusive* access to the information that shows the overall picture. Computers allow information to be available to a greater number of people almost instantaneously so that decisions can be based on concrete facts and can be made by any number of people throughout the organization.

Within the world of factories, computer-integrated manufacturing systems (CIM) have been developed to link engineering, production, and marketing into one informational system. As these systems are perfected, the managers who now perform this linking function might be expendable. In fact, one reason for implementing CIM systems is to automate the flow of information through a factory so that indirect labor costs, including middle management costs, can be cut.

Some say that new technologies may be shrinking the numbers of all middle-wage jobs. Those who have sounded the alarm for the "vanishing middle" in the workforce have predicted that technology will lead to an increase in high-wage, high-skill professional positions as well as an increase in low-wage, low-skill jobs. The jobs that are viewed as being most expendable are the semiskilled jobs in the middle of the wage continuum. This argument is based on the theory that the jobs that pay minimum wages are not worth automating while the higher-level analytical jobs cannot be automated. Therefore, the high payoff for companies would come from automating predictable, repetitive, and relatively high-paying jobs such as welding or insurance claims adjustment. Demand within both of these occupations has dwindled due to automation (Hodgkinson 1986).

Opponents of this view of the "vanishing middle" argue that the types of jobs that are disappearing in manufacturing industries have been low paying. They cite examples from the textiles and clothing industries where predominantly low-skill jobs filled primarily by women have been eliminated as machines have moved in. They also maintain that the loss of the middle-wage manufacturing jobs is being offset by middle-wage jobs in fast-growing service industries such as business and health services. For example, the demand for occupational therapists, dieticians, accountants, auditors, and computer programmers has risen.

Technology Affects Skills Requirements

Although the experts often disagree about how technology affects occupational demand, everyone agrees that technology will affect the skills required within many occupations. However, some have argued that technology is increasing the skill and education requirements for the workforce, while others maintain that jobs are actually becoming deskilled. A report issued by the Office of Technology Assessment (1986) argued that both positions are overly simplified. Machines alone do not dictate the design of jobs or the skills required to perform those jobs. When new machines and processes are introduced into the workplace, managers and engineers decide how to organize human tasks in relationship to the technology. According to the report, these decisions

> determine whether the new jobs are deskilled or upgraded, whether they contain variety or are narrow and repetitious, whether they involve broader responsibilities or are confined to an isolated aspect of the firm's business, and possibly whether they provide opportunities for growth and advancement for better jobs.

In support of this position, the report cited examples of how jobs have been upgraded or deskilled when the same technology was introduced in different companies. Thus, the combination of job design and new equipment contributes to the level and nature of skill requirements.

Job Design and Skills Requirements

Although no one has a perfect design for combining machines and people, some common trends in job design are emerging. For instance, as sophisticated microprocessor systems are introduced into the workplace, power and responsibility tend to be pushed down through the organization. Upper-level managers relinquish some of the control that they wielded in the traditional pyramidal organization, and people at all levels within the company make more decisions concerning their work and how to do it. Thus, workers need the skills that allow them to make sound decisions and to feel comfortable with increased responsibility and control.

In the move toward increasing employee responsibility and control, many companies have started various forms of employee involvement programs, ranging from quality circles to participatory management. According to a recent government study, close to half of American companies with over 100 employees have participative management programs that bring workers and supervisors together. For example, both General Motors and Ford Motors have a variety of employee involvement programs that are jointly run by union and management and that involve employees in decision making and problem solving in their work areas (Wise 1985). They are designed to improve the quality of work life and to increase productivity. Indeed, productivity increases heavily depend on "human

Job Design and Skills Requirements

factors" such as employee suggestions (Office of Technology Assessment 1986; Driscoll 1979). If these programs are to be effective, employees need to be able to provide managers with useful information. Because many of the programs rely on problem-solving teams, employees also need to know how to be good team members and team leaders. As a member of a quality circle in a manufacturing setting told me, "Through our quality circle training, I've learned to listen to the other guy's ideas, even if they sound silly at first. I used to be pretty bull-headed about pushing my ideas without hearing the other guy out."

This tendency to involve employees in small group problem solving is indicative of another major organizational trend—establishing collaborative work environments. Computer networks connect workers to each other in new ways. If the new technology is to lead to increased productivity, people must learn to coordinate their activities. Management consultant Stephen Rosenthal offers an example of the problems companies run into when computers bring together people who are not used to working closely with one another. He describes a company that spent $23 million for computer-aided design and computer-aided manufacturing equipment. Half of the equipment went to engineers while the other half went to manufacturing personnel, but because the company forgot to teach the two groups to communicate with each other, their efforts were not coordinated and the company reaped few benefits from the new equipment (Hymovitz 1985).

In the future, computer-integrated manufacturing systems (CIM) will combine electronic communications, data-based management, decision-support analyses, and automated equipment. People from design, manufacturing, marketing, sales, and financial groups will need to understand how their job functions interconnect and how to communicate with each other. In these information-intensive environments, production supervisors exchange data constantly with engineers, systems operators, and maintenance workers. Likewise, maintenance crews must work closely with production floor people because integrated systems are complex, diagnosing problems is difficult, and people on the plant floor are in the best position to note early symptoms of potential problems.

Many highly automated factories depend on multiskilled, collaborative production teams. This popular job design requires several individuals with varying skills and backgrounds to work together. Team members usually learn several jobs and rotate the performance of tasks. The team frequently assumes all or some of the activities of the supervisor or foreman such as allocating work, controlling absenteeism, and coordinating activities with other departments (Office of Technology Assessment 1986). Volvo, the Scandinavian auto company, has used the team approach to production for a decade. Volvo employees work in groups, rotate job assignments, and vary their work pace. Similarly, Saab, another Swedish automaker, began using teams in the 1970s. Within Saab, many service functions that previously had been performed outside of production departments have been incorporated into the roles of the blue-collar teams. As the technological systems used to produce the cars become more complex, the boundaries between blue-collar and white-collar work continue to shift. Currently, the blue-collar teams include more and more indirect responsibilities such as robot maintenance and programming (Malotke 1985).

Within recent years, the multiskilled team approach to job design has become more popular within the United States. Ford Motor Company eliminated the traditional organizational structure for producing the Taurus and the Mercury Sable. The cars were designed and produced through a team of representatives from planning, design, engineering, and manufacturing. These automobiles have been referred to as "the hottest U.S. cars in years." The team approach was so successful that Ford has decided to try team management throughout the company (Mitchell 1986). Another U.S. manufacturer that is experimenting with the team concept for producing automobiles is General Motors. The 6,000 production workers employed at the new Saturn plant in Springhill, Tennessee, have been organized into teams without foremen. The team members participate in making almost all decisions pertaining to their work (Choate and Linger 1986). A manager of Business Planning and Systems Integration at Saturn Corporation summed up the philosophy behind this approach to job design: "Instead of only a few people being paid to think and the rest being paid for their bodies from the neck down, everyone's ideas are needed to work on developing and applying new technology and on improving existing methods and approaches to remain competitive" (Wise 1985).

Job Design and Skills Requirements

Companies that use multiskilled teams usually value employee motivation, loyalty, and commitment. In keeping with a philosophy that the company's health depends on qualified and committed employees, they frequently provide more training than do traditional companies. One of the goals of training is to help employees understand how they personally contribute to the corporate goals.

These companies are also likely to organize around products rather than functions. They believe that employees are more likely to take personal pride in their work when they can identify with a particular product rather than merely perform fragmented tasks. Work is organized so that individual workers assemble entire units rather than merely add a piece to a unit. Usually this type of work organization requires all workers to have more knowledge and skills. In many cases, work teams not only assemble whole products but also are involved in planning, inspection, and quality control. As an employee who works on a production team put it, "I never get careless. I feel like I am responsible for making sure that the cars run right—and there is always something new to learn so I don't get bored."

Offices have been slower to adopt the collaborative team approach to work design, but new work configurations are likely to increase as computer systems and networks prevail in offices. Similar to the factory, routine work in offices can become so fragmented and simplified that employees lose motivation and become less productive. The tradeoff is that nonroutine work is often demanding. If employees are asked to perform more complex tasks, they must have the skills to meet that challenge.

Collaborative work environments require new attitudes and skills throughout a company. As employees take on greater responsibilities for solving problems and making decisions, they must be competent in basic skills such as reading, writing, and math. Moreover, because computers connect people to one another in new ways, employees need to understand how their work fits into the whole. Neither individuals nor departments can afford to be territorial and protective of their work. Turf battles have to give way to commitment to shared goals. The team approach to work requires skills in group problem solving, conflict management, communication skills, and leadership skills.

Technical Skills

New technologies directly affect the technical skill requirements for the workplace of the future. However, forecasting the specific skills likely to be required for future technologies is difficult because predictions of technological innovations are imprecise. Some innovations have occurred more slowly than forecasters have anticipated, while others have occurred more quickly than expected. Moreover, once the technology is available, its use depends on unforeseeable factors such as economic conditions, consumer preferences, and management strategies (Office of Technology Assessment 1986).

One approach to forecasting specific skill requirements is to analyze the occupations that are created by new technologies. For example, the use of robotics in factories creates a need for robotics technicians who maintain and repair the machines. These technicians need a strong foundation in high school–level math, blueprint reading, basic mechanics, basic electronics, and other equipment-specific application skills (Zemke 1983). This type of skills analysis can provide useful, yet limited, information about job requirements because estimates of the demand for such occupations are often inaccurate. For example, in the early 1980s forecasters projected a tremendous proliferation of industrial robots and, consequently, a need for large numbers of robot technicians. In fact, robot use has not grown outside of the automotive industry, and the projected need for robot technicians proved to be inflated.

Although specific technical skill requirements are difficult to predict, general skill needs can be forecast quite accurately. Experts agree that the future workplace will need more multiskilled generalists than specialists. For example, engineers will need electronic and mechanical backgrounds due to the overlay of mechanical, electrical, and electronic systems in current and future factories, and computer specialists will need knowledge of both hardware and software.

Microprocessor technology leads to a shift from physical activity to mental effort. In the airplane industry riveting, a semiskilled production job, involves fastening together the fuselage and wings of planes. The job used to be done with a hand-held riveting gun, but now a numerically controlled riveting machine has replaced

Technical Skills

the manual labor. The computer establishes the correct position and procedures for driving the rivets; the operator has no physical contact with the work but observes the process on a television screen, watches for errors, and does some troubleshooting. These changes are not limited to making airplanes. In many modern factories, the production process is computerized so that people are no longer involved in the physical execution of tasks but are responsible for monitoring the automated processes and making judgments pertaining to the entire operation. Of course, this shift from physical to mental creates new sources of error. The people who work with the new technologies must understand the entire production process and must become adept at spotting unusual events that might signal potential problems. Automated systems sometimes malfunction in unpredictable ways. The operator's main function is to notice, interpret, and respond to unexpected errors in the process. Every time the process breaks down, operators must learn from their experiences and adjust the way they attend to and interpret information. They are continuously called on to learn and adapt. The people who operate these systems must be vigilant to patterns in the information that they monitor and must be able to quickly respond to any unexpected changes in the process. In fact, the human operators become more important with sophisticated technologies because even one unexpected event can lead to the breakdown of an entire production process. The organization therefore becomes highly dependent on the operators' interpretations and judgments to prevent costly shutdowns.

Because of the frequency with which technological innovations occur, workers will be called on to continuously acquire new skills. Training and retraining will become business as usual. In *Future Shock*, Alvin Toffler (1970) argues that the illiterate of the year 2000 will not be those who cannot read but those who cannot learn. Some companies are already raising the skill requirements for entry-level workers. Banks and other financial institutions are examples of this trend. The president of a large multistate bank recently justified new hiring policies by explaining that "everyone working within the banking industry at every level must be prepared to adapt to new methods, new products, and new technologies quickly and constantly." Because ability to learn hinges on a sound foundation in basic skills, the required level of proficiency in reading, mathematics, problem solving, and communications skills will increase.

Technology Affects the Nature of Work

Computers not only affect the skills required to perform jobs but change the very nature of work. The shift from dependence on physical skills to dependence on mental processes means that work becomes less tangible. An increasing number of jobs require the scanning, selecting, and mental processing of abstract symbols via computer terminals. Examples range from the continuous process operator in the factory who monitors information from visual displays and no longer actually checks vat levels to the bill collector who works with "on-line real time systems" rather than with account cards (Zuboff 1981). Even within the health professions, the hands-on aspects of work have dwindled. In hospital laboratories, medical technologists test blood and other body fluids for disease-producing organisms. Formerly, they worked with equipment such as pipettes and bottled reactants. Now the technologists merely determine which test the computer will perform and make judgments concerning the validity of the results (Office of Technology Assessment 1986). Likewise, nurses now can keep track of the vital signs of patients by monitoring remote computer terminals rather than by visiting each patient's room and manually applying the equipment to check pulse, temperature, and so forth.

Regardless of whether people welcome or regret the changes, work has been transformed. An employee at a peanut butter plant described how his work had improved as a result of automation. He had been involved in checking the peanut roasters for approximately twenty years. When he first began checking roasters, the work required him to actually climb to the top of these large machines to check temperatures as well as other process indicators; currently he uses a computer to monitor the roasters. He laughed as he talked about his fears when the computers were installed: "I wasn't sure I'd like my job when the computers were doing it for me. But, man, was I wrong! I don't miss climbing up to the top of those hot roasters at all! Now I can stay in the air-conditioned control room and do my job with no sweat." This is one case where the employee welcomed the disappearance of the hands-on aspect of his work.

On the other hand, sometimes these changes feel strange to employees. A secretary who had moved from typewriters to word processors to personal computers hooked into a mainframe system said that she felt like she got much more work done now but, in some ways, felt less productive because she could not always put her hands on her work at the end of the day. "I almost feel like my typing has disappeared when I turn off the computer. Don't get me wrong—I don't want to go back to the typewriter! It's just that some days I can't tell you how much I've accomplished because I can't point to the pages." In his book *Beyond Mechanization*, Larry Hirschhorn characterized this change from the industrial to the postindustrial workplace as a dramatic transformation in the relationship between work and consciousness. The prototypical industrial semiskilled worker was chained to his tool, but his mind was free to wander. Now the worker is removed from the physical execution of the work, but he must remain vigilant in monitoring processes and is therefore mentally chained to the work (Hirschhorn, 1984).

Changing Skills for Managers

When technology changes pervade an organization, managers are not immune from their effects. If people at lower levels in the organization acquire greater responsibility, management style must become less controlling and more facilitative. Managers become delegators, coaches, and motivators. Although this role comes easily to some managers, others have a difficult time adjusting. These changes are likely to be particularly significant for first-line managers in companies with work teams. The boundaries between workers and managers are less distinct in these organizations. In fact, first-line managers often switch from directing people to managing technical information. They tend to rely heavily on their work groups for the daily flow of technical information. In these situations, upper-level managers need to clarify the first-line manager's reponsibilities and provide appropriate guidance and training for the new roles.

If this guidance and training are not provided, the first-line supervisors' actions are likely to become ineffective at best or counterproductive at worst. For example, a large communications company reorganized and restructured its work approaches a few years ago. The company developed a semi-autonomous team approach for installing and servicing telecommunication systems. Unfortunately, first-line supervisors became openly rebellious when the company failed to help them redefine their roles and learn new management styles that would fit those roles. Instead of becoming facilitative, some supervisors pulled in the reins even more tightly on the employees and became more controlling and demanding. They were confused about their roles and struggled to hold on to their power base in a situation where the distribution of power had shifted. Ultimately, they prevented the teams from functioning effectively. The problem was finally corrected when upper-level officials in the company recognized that first-line supervisors needed to be resocialized and retrained.

The facilitative management style calls for strong interpersonal and communication skills, skills that are also required for the new networking style of management. As computers link processes together, people exchange information horizontally across the organization: Everyone becomes a resource to everyone else. The role of the manager is to create a supportive environment in which this communication and sharing can take place. Because managers become mentors for employees and developers of human potential, communication and other interpersonal skills become crucial tools for effective management. This emphasis on "people" skills is a particularly significant transition for manufacturing managers because historically their training has focused more on technical than interpersonal skills (Lynch and Orne 1985). Nevertheless, exceptional interpersonal skills will be crucial for managers in the factory of the future as they become the links between the workforce, suppliers, and subcontractors, both within the United States and abroad.

The facilitative, strongly interpersonal style of management has always been successful in service industries. The traditional directive style has never worked well within service companies because of their high concentration of professional, scientific, and technical employees. These people learn to be self-reliant and independent through their professional training and, as a result, do not respond well to a controlling type of management. Furthermore, the nature of service transactions is more conducive to the facilitative management style. Because a direct relationship often exists between the server and the client, the server must rely on individual judgment when delivering the service. Direct supervision of such service transactions is impractical if not impossible. A restaurant supervisor can directly neither control nor manage each interaction between waiters and customers. Likewise, the manager in a consulting firm cannot directly supervise the day-to-day interactions between consultants and their clients. The best method for ensuring quality in the provision of services is through the training and motivation of individual employees—a philosophy that is consistent with the facilitative model of management.

As the economy depends more on technology and is more dominated by service industries, the skills required for management change. It is not always easy for some managers to accept that the new model of management is facilitative rather than controlling. The general manager of a recently redesigned food processing plant admitted to me,

> I know that I have to loosen up. My managers have to be left alone to make their own decisions. I can't order them around any more. They have to make quicker decisions than before, and I can't always be there to give them advice and directions. And yet I've managed this operation forcefully for 20 years. I don't know if I can change.

As Lyman Ketchum (who helped redesign jobs for Gaines Foods) has pointed out, accepting this new model of management requires the old-style bureaucrats to go through a "personal paradigm shift which is a deep psychological process" (Hoerr, Pollack, and Whiteside 1986).

Although people skills are becoming increasingly important to the manager's role, expanded technical skills also will be required for successful management. As decision-making responsibility is pushed down throughout the organization, managers are frequently in the position of having to make decisions that include judgments about science and technology. Furthermore, as workers solve more of their own work problems, the issues brought to managers are those that workers cannot resolve on their own. These problems are likely to require higher-level scientific and technical training in areas such as equipment maintenance and operation. Noted economist Eli Ginzberg (1985) has pointed out that scientists cannot fulfill their roles as managers merely on the basis of their scientific knowledge. Moreover, managers are very often unqualified to make decisions that require knowledge of science and technology. He recommends broadening the educational base of both groups.

The ability to use computers is a technical skill that has emerged as crucial to management. Managers can no longer afford to view the computer as clerical equipment because computer literacy is becoming a prerequisite to advancement. As a 1985 headline in the *Wall Street Journal* proclaimed, "Rising stars can become obsolete has-beens if they can't come to grips with the computer" (Roth 1985). At the very least, managers must master computer literacy so that they can oversee the work of their staff. Moreover, by using the computer, managers can become more objective and base their decisions on data rather than mere intuition. In order to effectively use the information that the computer provides, managers need strong conceptual skills that allow them to ask the right questions and to identify the data that address those questions. Unless framed within the context of clear issues, information becomes not only useless but overwhelming.

Manufacturing managers as a group face sharply increasing demands on their time and conceptual abilities. They not only will need to be computer literate but also will need to learn new skills and knowledge related to computer technology, such as computer-aided design and computer-aided manufacturing, group technology, flexible manufacturing systems, just-in-time inventory control, manufacturing resource planning, and robotics. At the same time that the skill requirements for manufacturing managers are on the rise, however, so are managers' status and importance.

The Role of Corporate Culture

Sometimes the changes brought about by technology challenge the basic beliefs and value systems within traditional organizations. Some critics have argued that technology cannot pay for itself without fomenting a social revolution at work (Hoerr, Pollack, and Whiteside 1986). Indeed, computer technologies often force changes in corporate cultures, and an effective retraining process must consider these beliefs and value systems. Simply teaching people new technical skills does not always ensure that they will make successful transitions.

Corporate cultures are those shared values and beliefs that operate within a company. These cultures often influence company strategies as well as the way employees relate to each other. Actually, most companies tend to be composed of a conglomeration of occupational subcultures: Engineers may share one set of values, clerical staff another set, and the salesforce still another. In addition, companies usually have an overall culture that pervades the entire organization. Individuals are socialized into the company culture when first hired and are resocialized whenever they make any major move—whether they move to a new function, a new location, or a new position. The need to resocialize individuals who move within the company is dramatically magnified when an entire organization undergoes a transition. The introduction of sophisticated microprocessor technology forces such a transformation on the organization. The changes in the nature of work with the accompanying changes in job design, skill requirements, and organizational structure often clash with the core values and beliefs that historically pervaded the company. These collisions between technology-induced social changes and long-standing corporate cultures can lead to the failure of otherwise strong corporate strategies. According to Edgar Schein (1985), many companies have devised strategic plans that were sound from a financial, product, or marketing perspective but that failed because they were inconsistent with the organization's basic assumptions.

In addition to interacting with the overall organizational culture, technology can affect subcultures within a company. For instance, people within occupations frequently develop views of themselves that are strongly related to the nature of the technology they use to perform their work. Nurses who monitor the vital signs of the patients by visiting each patient's room and manually applying equipment to check pulses and temperatures undoubtedly view their role differently than do the nurses who monitor vital signs from a remote computer terminal. Likewise, draftsmen who use pencils and drawing boards to draw, shade, and color are likely to perceive their craft differently than draftsmen who combine blocks and shapes electronically through a keyboard and screen. As the activities associated with work become more homogeneous across occupations, the craft or unique skills that distinguish one job from another disappear. An increasingly large proportion of tasks in the workplace are performed in front of computer terminals.

In addition to affecting workers' self-definitions, the introduction of technology often influences the power and status of occupational groups. With the advent of computer-assisted design systems, engineers can often release their own sketches rather than rely on draftsmen to perform this activity. As engineers grow less dependent on draftsmen, draftsmen, in turn, may feel that their importance to the company is diminished. To a great extent, power comes from access to information. Because computers make information available to more people at lower levels within the organization, the responsibility for decision making is likely to be redistributed. Traditional power bases will frequently be disrupted, an event that is likely to shake an organizational culture. If not adequately addressed, the potential for such shifts can lead to resistance to the new technologies, which are often accurately viewed as driving the social changes.

As technologies lead to organizational transformations, company leaders should assess how these changes affect the operational corporate culture. These assessments are likely to uncover potential clashes with the organization's established social system. Astute business leaders clarify and redefine roles in an overall strategy for introducing the new technologies. Once new role definitions are clear, strategists can identify the skills and attitudes required to perform those roles. Only then can comprehensive and effective retraining strategies be devised. In addition to the traditional methods of skills acquisition, comprehensive retraining strategies must include a mechanism for resocializing people into new roles.

Summary and Implications

The changing skill requirements for the workplace of the future have serious implications for retraining programs. Almost all jobs, from production to management, will require a strong foundation in basic skills such as reading, mathematics, reasoning, and communicating. Many members of the American workforce are not currently proficient in these skills, however, and furthermore, the

Summary and Implications

people who enter the workforce in the next decade are likely to be less proficient in these basic skills.

The Center for Public Resources published a report entitled *Basic Skills in the U.S. Workforce* (1982) that was based on a national survey of corporations, school systems, and trade unions. It concluded that American businesses are already struggling with problems that stem from the basic skill deficiencies that prevail in the labor force. The lack of sound basic skills limits job advancement of employees and hinders companies' productivity. In focusing on workplace requirements, the survey results were consistent with other studies. In general, the respondents representing businesses indicated that medium-level competencies in reading, writing, and reasoning and medium-to-high competencies in mathematics are already required for many jobs in most industries. Likewise, they felt that medium and high levels of communications skills are needed for all job categories in all industries. A basic to medium-level understanding of science was thought to be important even for entry-level secretarial and supervisory positions, as well as for technical and higher-level management jobs. Corporate, school, and union respondents alike emphasized the importance of high-level "human relations" and "work behavior" skills as necessary for most jobs.

In specifically addressing where the current workforce stands in meeting the workplace skill requirements, most corporations surveyed identified skill deficiencies in most job categories. Of particular significance are the respondents' comments concerning inadequacies in reasoning abilities. They identified secretarial, technical, and supervisory personnel as showing the greatest deficiencies and noted that poor problem-solving ability greatly hinders the success of their retraining efforts. People who cannot think in hypothetical terms are unlikely to be able to apply what they learn in the classroom to real work problems. Likewise, concrete thinkers are hindered in generalizing the knowledge they gain from one type of job or experience to another; they are unable to apply facts to new circumstances. This mental inflexibility can prevent them from successfully retraining.

The business respondents showed great concern for the inadequacies in speaking and listening in both the skilled and unskilled labor force. The deficiencies showed up in inabilities to follow instructions and to express ideas verbally. These inadequacies are likely to become severe impediments as work relationships become more complex and interdependent.

The skill deficiencies in the current workforce are especially alarming in light of the trends for the future workplace. From the employee's point of view, basic skill inadequacies will prevent job advancement and cause tremendous vulnerability to skill obsolescence and possible unemployment. People who are illiterate and incompetent in mathematics will find retraining to be almost impossible. From the corporation's point of view, these deficiencies will affect general productivity, product quality, worker safety, and the amount of management or supervision time that must be invested in employees.

The ability of U.S. corporations to compete in the world economy is threatened by a workforce with inadequate skills. To survive companies must develop comprehensive strategies for retraining all kinds of workers at every level within the company, including management. The strategies must take into account basic interpersonal and technical skill requirements as well as the socialization process that will produce a proficient workforce for the future workplace.

References

Center for Public Resources. 1982. *Basic Skills in the U.S. Workforce*. Vol. 51, New York.

Choate, P., and J. K. Linger, 1986. *The High Flex Society*. New York: Alfred A. Knopf.

Driscoll, J. W. 1979. *Office Automation: The Organizational Redesign of Office Work*. CISR WP #15, Sloan WP #1064–79. Cambridge, Mass.: MIT Press.

Ginzberg, E. 1985. *Understanding Human Resources, Perceptives People and Policy*. Lanham, Md. University Press of America.

Hirschhorn, L. 1984. *Beyond Mechanization: Work and Technology in a Post-Industrial Age*. Cambridge, Mass.: MIT Press, p. 107.

Hodgkinson, H. L. 1986. *Future Search: A Look at the Present*. NEA Tec. Rep. Washington, D.C.: National Education Association, Professional and Organizational Development/Office of Planning.

Hoerr, J., M. Pollack, and D. E. Whiteside. 1986. "Management Discovers the Human Side of Automation." *Business Week* (September 29) p. 72.

Hymowitz, C. 1985. "Manufacturing Change: Automation Experts Explore

References

the Promise and Problems of the Factory of the Future." *Wall Street Journal*, A Special Report: Technology in the Workplace, September 16.

James, H., and J. Raymond. 1982. *Basic Skills in the U.S. Work Force.* New York: Center for Public Resources.

Lynch, J., and D. Orne. 1985. "The New Elite: Manufacturing Super-Managers." *Management Review* (April).

Malotke, J. F. 1985. "Automation and Its Impact on the Labor Force and the GM-UAW Saturn Project." *Labor Law Journal* (August).

Mills, P. K. 1986. *Managing Service Industries Organizational Practices in a Post-Industrial Economy.* Cambridge, Mass.: Ballinger.

Mitchell, R. 1986. "How Ford Hit the Bull's-Eye with Taurus." *Business Week* (June 30).

Office of Technology Assessment. 1985. *Automation of America's Offices, 1986–2000.* OTA No:287 p. 350. Washington, D.C.: USGPO.

———. 1986. *Technology and Structural Unemployment: Reemploying Displaced Adults.* OTA No:052–003–01017–8. Washington, D.C.: USGPO.

Perelman, L. J. 1985. *Safety Lines vs. Safety Nets: Why MADMUPS Need Help.* Paper presented at National Conference of State Legislators' Workshop on Resources for Dislocated Workers, Washington, D.C., September 5.

Roth, T. 1985. "Finished at Forty: Rising Stars Can Become Obsolete Has-Beens If They Can't Come to Grips with the Computer." *Wall Street Journal*, A Special Report: Technology in the Workplace, September 16.

Rumberger, R. W. 1986. *The Changing Industrial Structure of the U.S. Economy: Its Impact on the Employment Earnings and Educational Requirements of Jobs.* Tec Rep, 86–SP1–8. Palo Alto, Calif.: Standard University, Education Policy Institute (July).

Schein, E. H. 1985. *Organizational Culture and Leadership.* San Francisco: Jossey-Bass.

Snyder, D. P. 1984. *The Strategic Context of Management in America 1985–1995.* Bethesda, Md.: Snyder Family Enterprise.

Toffler, Alvin. 1970. *Future Shock.* New York: Random House.

Wise, E. E. 1985. New Technology and Labor-Management Relations at Ford Motor Company. *Labor Law Journal* (August).

Zemke, R. 1983. "The Robots Are Coming! Training Tomorrow's High-Tech Workers." *Training: The Magazine of Human Resources Development* (June) p. 576.

Zuboff, S. 1981. *Psychological and Organizational Implications of Computer-Mediated Work.* CISR No. 71 Sloan W.P. #1224–81. Cambridge, Mass.: MIT Press.

CHAPTER THREE

◆

Sharing the Challenge:
Partnerships for Retraining

IN ORDER to address the greatly expanding need for updating the skills of people in the workforce, corporations have increased their education and training efforts dramatically in recent years. Employers provide their employees with remedial education as well as sophisticated technical training. The need for training in the workplace has become so widespread that corporations are joining with government agencies and labor unions to plan, pay for, and administer programs. Likewise, educational institutions are entering new relationships with businesses to assist with the development and delivery of training and retraining. The programs that result from these new partnerships demonstrate what can be done when groups are willing to form alliances to attack problems.

Overview of Workplace Training

Workplace training has grown so dramatically over the last decade that it now matches the size of public education in the United States. In fact, the formal corporate education industry is currently over a $30 billion enterprise, and an additional $180 billion goes into informal employee training. Employers now train as many as 40 million people a year (Carnevale 1986). These numbers account for the reference to workplace-based training as the "second system of post-secondary education" (Hodgkinson 1986).

Although the corporate education industry is undeniably large, the services are not equally available to everyone. Training opportunities are unevenly distributed across industries, occupations, and age groups. In general, institutions with large numbers of highly skilled employees (such as federal government agencies) or highly specialized industries (such as banking, insurance, and real estate) tend to be large providers of training. Predictably, large organizations provide more training than do their smaller counterparts. Furthermore, the employees within those large companies who are most likely to receive formal training are twenty-five- to forty-four-year-old, white-collar managers, professionals, or salespersons. Blue-collar employees are not without training opportunities, but they are more likely to receive informal, on-the-job instruction (Gordon 1987).

Clearly training is a common activity in the modern workplace. Companies vary considerably in who gets trained, however, as well as in what gets taught. Some companies train only for the acquisition of technical skills, whereas others offer a wide range of topics including some personal development subjects. The favored areas for instruction include management, technical, and communication skills (Lee 1987). Tables 3–1 to 3–4 illustrate in detail the types and sizes of industries that provide training, the classes of employees that are usually trained, and the types of training those employees receive.

Although all evidence points to the need for a workforce that is strong in basic skills such as reading, writing, and math, this remedial education is addressed by only a small percentage of employers, which is unfortunate because employees who cannot read and write at reasonable levels are not likely to benefit from any other formal training programs.

Remedial Education

As companies plan strategies for retraining their employees, many will find that they must address the need for remedial education before proceeding with any other form of instruction. Although in the past relatively little emphasis has been placed on basic skills training in the workplace, a growing number of companies now sponsor remedial education programs for their workers. In fact, a 1987 survey prepared by *Training Magazine* indicated that 18.8 percent of the respondent corporations with fifty or more employees

Table 3–1: Who Gets the Training

Job Category	Organizations Providing Training (%)[a]	Mean Number of Individuals Trained[b]	Projected Number of Individuals Trained[c] (in millions)	Mean Number of Hours Delivered[d]	Projected Total Hours of Training Delivered[e] (in millions)
Salespeople	32.7	40.4	3.26	42.6	138.8
Middle managers	73.8	17.2	3.13	36.6	114.6
Executives	70.4	5.4	.94	36.3	34.0
Professionals	48.1	49.8	5.91	35.8	211.4
Senior managers	56.1	9.8	1.36	33.6	45.5
First-line supervisors	58.7	28.3	4.10	33.3	136.4
Production workers	26.9	130.6	8.66	29.1	252.1
Customer service people	39.6	60.0	5.86	26.8	157.0
Administrative employees	50.5	18.1	2.25	21.8	49.1
Office/clerical	52.5	26.0	3.37	16.9	56.9
Total			38.82		1,195.8

a. Percentage of all U.S. organizations with fifty or more employees that provide training to people in these categories.
b. Average number of individuals trained per organization, based only on those organizations that do provide some training.
c. Total number of people trained in all organizations (in millions).
d. Average hours of training per individual, based only on organizations that do provide some training.
e. Total trainee-hours of training delivered by all organizations to all employees in these categories (in millions).

Remedial Education

Table 3–2: General Types of Training

Types of Training	% Providing[a]	In-House Only (%)[b]	Outside Only (%)[c]	Both (%)[d]
Management skills/development	78.5	11.8	20.5	46.2
Supervisory skills	69.3	35.9	8.5	24.9
Communication skills	66.3	18.5	13.3	34.5
Technical skills/knowledge	65.0	21.2	5.1	38.7
Executive development	57.8	7.2	21.0	29.6
Clerical/secretarial skills	56.7	16.5	15.9	24.3
New methods/procedures	56.5	32.3	3.1	21.1
Customer relations/services	55.3	20.5	8.7	26.1
Computer literacy/basic computer skills	51.2	29.3	6.0	15.9
Personal growth	49.1	13.1	13.1	22.9
Sales skills	40.2	14.8	6.0	19.4
Employee/labor relations	39.9	14.3	9.6	16.0
Disease prevention/health promotion	37.6	15.5	7.6	14.5
Customer education	29.7	23.5	0.3	5.9
Remedial basic education	18.8	9.7	5.3	3.8

Of all organizations with fifty or more employees:
a. Percentage that provide each type of training.
b. Percentage that say all training of this type is designed and delivered by in-house staff.
c. Percentage that say all training of this type is designed and delivered by outside consultants or vendors.
d. Percentage that say training of this type is designed and delivered by a combination of in-house staff and outside vendors.

Table 3–3: General Types of Training by Industry[a]

Types of Training	Manufacturing	Transportation/ Communications/ Utilities	Wholesale/ Retail Trade	Finance/ Insurance/ Banking	Business Services	Health Services	Educational Services	Public Administration	All Industries
Management skills/ development	79.4	63.7	79.2	78.3	80.0	92.8	71.0	85.1	**78.5**
Supervisory skills	63.7	57.6	71.1	79.0	64.3	71.8	61.0	84.4	**69.3**
Communication skills	61.6	61.5	61.2	65.1	61.5	91.6	63.7	81.9	**66.3**
Technical skills/ knowledge	57.4	68.3	62.2	70.8	53.9	74.4	52.8	82.5	**65.0**
Executive development	49.0	53.7	51.8	49.7	62.9	79.0	65.3	73.3	**57.8**
Clerical/secretarial skills	41.5	60.3	65.5	52.9	52.6	65.6	66.1	74.6	**56.7**
New methods/ procedures	37.3	54.5	60.7	65.9	53.1	76.6	46.8	66.1	**56.5**
Customer relations/services	37.8	65.2	81.0	77.0	46.9	71.7	33.4	30.4	**55.3**
Computer literacy/ basic computer skills	36.5	58.4	44.3	51.4	51.0	39.7	66.3	71.4	**51.2**
Personal growth	33.9	44.0	51.5	45.1	51.9	62.4	60.3	59.8	**49.1**
Sales skills	45.6	29.4	69.7	59.3	38.0	31.2	19.3	3.3	**40.2**

Table 3–3: General Types of Training by Industry[a] (continued)

Types of Training	Manufac- turing	Transpor- tation/ Communi- cations/ Utilities	Wholesale/ Retail Trade	Finance/ Insurance/ Banking	Business Services	Health Services	Educa- tional Services	Public Adminis- tration	All Indus- tries
Employee/labor relations	39.3	44.6	30.2	35.4	39.3	58.4	33.1	51.8	39.9
Disease prevention/ health promotion	36.3	37.9	32.8	25.9	34.6	74.9	43.9	43.1	37.6
Customer education	33.4	41.9	52.5	27.5	28.1	41.1	20.7	7.3	29.7
Remedial basic education	30.6	26.4	22.6	13.6	11.3	9.9	29.9	12.9	18.8

a. Percentage of all organizations within each industry that offer these types of training.

Table 3–4: General Types of Training by Size of Organization[a]

Types of Training	50–99	100–499	500–999	1,000–2,499	2,500–9,999	10,000 or More
Management skills/development	75.0	79.8	83.7	88.9	91.3	87.4
Supervisory skills	68.5	66.9	75.3	77.7	82.2	77.3
Communication skills	61.1	68.0	75.0	78.1	84.9	84.2
Technical skills/knowledge	57.4	72.3	70.7	80.3	76.4	85.2
Executive development	54.6	57.0	63.3	70.3	70.0	76.3
New methods/procedures	53.7	56.8	62.0	64.2	63.2	67.2
Clerical/secretarial skills	50.9	59.0	63.7	68.1	68.3	69.4
Customer relations/services	48.1	60.1	59.7	68.8	70.0	64.7
Computer literacy/basic computer skills	50.9	49.1	52.3	56.4	57.5	68.8
Personal growth	45.4	49.1	55.3	58.4	60.8	65.0
Employee/labor relations	35.2	42.0	42.3	53.1	57.0	62.8
Sales skills	35.2	43.5	39.3	45.6	49.5	54.3
Disease prevention/health promotion	33.3	38.9	46.0	53.6	50.5	50.2
Customer education	26.9	29.5	29.7	33.6	33.9	40.7
Remedial basic education	18.5	17.0	16.3	18.7	24.3	26.8

a. Percentage of organizations providing these types of training to employees.

currently provide some form of remedial education (Lee 1987). These companies have found that employees who cannot read and write exact high costs on employers in lost productivity, poor quality products, and accidents (Lee 1986). More and more employers are convinced that the cost of the remedial education is justified.

Companies frequently implement strategies for addressing basic skill deficiencies as they introduce new processes and technologies into the workplace. Executives in a large chemical manufacturing company reported that they discovered the reading and math deficiencies in their workforce when they attempted to introduce statistical quality control. Many employees did not have the basic reading levels and math proficiencies needed to perform the operations of systematically observing and recording simple data about the manufacturing process. Moreover, some of the employees could not comprehend the training materials.

The basic skill problem faced by this chemical company is not unique. When employers introduce new technology, they commonly discover that their employees cannot read. When Onan Corporation, a manufacturer of electric equipment and controls, introduced new automated equipment into the workplace, managers conducted a study of their employees' readiness for working with the new technology. They discovered that a large number of people with reading deficiencies could not even complete the questionnaire that asked them about their educational backgrounds. Moreover, many of them could not add fractions, perform long division, or compute averages. The company now spends $20,000 to $25,000 per year on an educational program that includes instruction in basics such as reading and math (Ross 1986).

Over the next few years more and more companies will look for strategies to address their employees' basic skill impairments. A few companies have long-standing programs that can serve as models for others. Polaroid Corporation has offered a remedial education program to employees since the 1960s. The company is so convinced of the program's value that even when financial problems forced a reduction in workforce a few years ago, the basic skills training stayed in place. Although the program serves many people, the instruction is tailored to each individual employee's learning needs as determined through a thorough skills assessment (Lee 1986). The program provides courses that cover topics such as basic reading and math, science, computers, problem solving, speaking, and listening.

More recently, General Motors and Ford Motors have developed large-scale corporate-sponsored basic skills training programs in cooperation with the United Auto Workers of America. Both corporations have packaged their remedial education efforts with more comprehensive, large-scale retraining programs. One good reason for this packaging is that adults are frequently too embarrassed to admit that they cannot read or perform basic mathematical operations and will not go to programs that are limited to basic skills instruction. They feel that participating in these programs stigmatizes them. If these classes are included in a broader curriculum and labeled as prerequisites for the higher-level courses, employees seem to be less reluctant to participate.

Companies report that the basic skills programs have paid off in terms of lower turnover, improved productivity, and enhanced trainability of employees. In fact, many employers conclude that they have little choice but to offer the remedial education. As one supervisor involved with a secretarial retraining program put it, "If they can't speak English and read, they can't train to be secretaries—and we can't find enough secretaries from the outside." This supervisor's dilemma is not uncommon. With the number of persons entering the workforce falling at the same time that skill requirements are increasing, employers face a serious challenge. They find that they depend more on their existing employees and therefore need a trainable workforce.

In an American Management Association briefing on "Workplace Literacy," Linda Stober from Polaroid Corporation made several recommendations to other companies that are considering establishing basic skills programs (Lee 1986). First, she advised companies to link their math and reading classes to their larger training goals. Second, although large corporations may be able to operate their own in-house programs, most medium and small companies do not have the resources to offer adequate basic skills programs without assistance and should contract for the services with an outside organization but work closely with the contractor to make sure that the training is on target. Finally, employers should address the issue of basic skills training within the context of their retraining strategies.

Occupational Retraining

Training employees is hardly a new activity within American corporations. Employers have always had to ensure that employees possess the skills needed to perform their jobs. The extent to which corporations are involved in *retraining*, however, is difficult to assess. When asked how they handle skill obsolescence in their workforce, most employers admit that they are more likely to hire new people than to switch their existing employees into new positions that require additional training. A widely quoted study of corporate retraining activities conducted by ITT Educational Services reported that a large percentage of *Fortune* 1500 companies retrain their employees to some extent (McClintock 1984), but this study considered all forms of training to be retraining. Far fewer employers conduct a significant amount of real retraining—the kind that leads to a different job or career for the employees involved. Although employers have always been concerned with maintaining a skilled workforce, their commitment to retraining has been limited: It is not the preferred method for addressing outdated occupations and skills. Furthermore, most of the retraining that does occur is informal and narrow in scope. This lack of interest in retraining is unfortunate because employers are in the best position to forecast their companies' skill needs and therefore to provide for the most effective upgrading of their own workforce.

Partnerships for Retraining

Most businesses prefer to conduct their own in-house training programs, but the retraining problem is so great that employers may opt to pool their efforts with unions, government, and educational institutions. Several collaborative ventures, usually referred to as *partnerships*, are already under way. They vary tremendously in scope as well as in focus. In some instances, the projects are large scale and long term, while in other cases, they are based on a short-term need. Some of the projects enroll workers who have been displaced by automation or who have been laid off because of changing business conditions; others help people upgrade their skills so that they can keep jobs with their present employers. These partnerships also vary in the nature of the association: The partners' commitments range from monetary to administrative assistance.

Government-Private Initiatives

All levels of government—from federal to state to local—are joining with private companies to address America's training needs. In general, the type of assistance that they bring to the partnership is financial and sometimes administrative.

Federal Programs. Currently the federal government provides retraining assistance through the Trade Adjustment and Assistance Program, the Carl Perkins Vocational Education Act, and the Job Training and Partnership Act. For the most part, all three programs are limited to displaced workers, defined as workers who have been laid off due to permanent plant closings.

The most extensive government assistance is provided through the Job Training and Partnership Act (JTPA), established by Congress in 1982. This act was intended to provide a mechanism through which the private sector could work cooperatively with the public sector to tailor training to the local job markets. The federal government provides funds to the states, which the states must match. In turn, the governor of each state establishes statewide objectives for job training and placement and determines who is eligible for assistance.

Local governments are involved through local Private Industry Councils (PICs), which are primarily responsible for developing and administering programs. The governor, however, has the authority to approve or disapprove the local training plans. The PICs consist primarily of representatives from the local business community, with some representatives from education, labor, economic development agencies, and public employment services. In cooperation with local government, the PICs decide who will administer the local programs and who will receive grant funds for local job training. In addition, each local PIC provides policy guidance and oversight of the job training for the local area.

Critics of JTPA are numerous. One objection is that it serves only a small fraction of the workers who are eligible for assistance. Another is that the programs funded through JTPA frequently emphasize immediately placing workers in new jobs rather than training them for long-term job security and career growth.

Until recently, most JTPA programs have been *reactive* rather than *proactive*. The programs often limit eligibility to workers who have already lost their jobs rather than assist the employed in upgrading their skills, but over the last two or three years more JTPA funds have been used to help companies retrain their own employees. Even so, these efforts have attracted widespread criticism by those who believe that federal and state money should be used to assist the unemployed rather than to subsidize businesses' training costs. The argument over who should pay for retraining goes on and on. Recently a task force established by the U.S. Department of Labor recommended stronger public-private joint commitments to funding retraining programs, with an emphasis on better methods for delivering services to displaced workers. The task force stressed that private-sector businesses must be stronger partners and take more initiative in retraining and that government programs for the displaced should complement and not replace efforts within the private sector. It recommended that the government-private partnerships tailor training to meet the specific needs of individual employers (Secretary of Labor's Task Force on Economic Adjustment and Worker Dislocation 1986).

The results of the task force's research indicated that the greatest number of people participate in retraining programs when the government provides money to companies to support internal projects. In addition, the data showed that these subsidies are most effective in firms that have had much previous experience in providing training. Thus government-private partnerships for retraining function best when the private partner is willing and knowledgeable enough to play a strong, active role in the retraining process.

State and Local Programs. Recently, many states and local governments have actively responded to economic changes by linking training policies and programs to their economic development efforts. These programs frequently attack the problems of worker displacement and unemployment in two ways: by providing assistance to businesses and by providing services directly to individuals. Some states have customized training programs that are tailored to meet the needs of specific businesses. Frequently the goal of this type of program is to help companies avoid shutting down due to lack of trained employees. Another way in which state and local governments assist businesses is to provide help with customized training programs for companies that are either expanding or redirecting their focus. A company may change its product line or its manufacturing technologies, which may affect the skill requirements of certain groups of employees. Under these circumstances, state and local governments may provide subsidies to employers to help with the training. The state of California, for example, has established a program for contributing funds to employers that want to upgrade their own workforces. This Community Work Site Education and Training program, as it is called, also helps with the development of skills within the general labor force. The goal for this program is to help people acquire the education and training that will match the long-range needs in the economy. The program receives money from the state general fund that is then funneled to an employer, a group of employers, or an industry to provide various types of training.

California has set up another retraining program called the Employment Training Panel. It assists businesses in implementing new technologies by providing them with suitably trained employees. This program retrains experienced white- or blue-collar workers who have either lost their jobs or are about to be displaced. The program prepares trainees for specific jobs. As a case in point, Hughes Aircraft was awarded $1 million to retrain over a thousand people to operate its new automated manufacturing system. Funding for this venture came from money that would normally go into the state's unemployment insurance program.

Another role that state and local agencies sometimes play is to serve as training coordinators and brokers. They help the businesses identify their training needs and then contact the groups or institutions that can provide the training. Several states, including Massachusetts and Kentucky, have state-funded skills corporations that bring together businesses in need of training assistance with prospective training providers. They also arrange for other services that businesses might desire such as recruitment, skills assessment, and customized training. Once the skills corporation makes the match between the business and an appropriate service provider, company managers work closely with the contractor to get the job done.

Partnerships for Retraining

They cooperate in the recruitment and selection of employees. They work together to carry out program details such as developing the training, constructing the curriculum, delivering the courses, counseling trainees, and overseeing placement.

In addition to connecting businesses with service providers, the skills corporations frequently award grants to educational institutions such as vocational schools and community colleges. The grant money is earmarked for the creation and expansion of programs to meet the needs of companies in the community. Usually they require that the money provided through grants must be matched by a contribution from the private sector.

Management-Labor Cooperation

Although training and employee development have not been significant collective bargaining issues in the past, unions and employers recently have shown great interest in these matters. The concern for these activities stems from an increasing urgency about job security.

As the pressures of global competition and widespread technological change mount, job protection and training issues crop up more frequently in collective bargaining agreements. Until now, training clauses have shown up primarily in accordances in the automotive and communications industries, although some activity has also occurred in the steel, construction, and service companies. Many of these labor contracts include provisions for joint union-management training and personal development programs. Most of these cooperative efforts are at least partially financed through company contributions based on a percentage of payroll or hours worked by the union employees. Some are limited to displaced or out-of-work employees, and others include skills upgrade training and retraining for active workers to help them *retain* employment. Frequently, the union-management partnerships also involve cooperation with federal, state, and community-based groups.

The UAW–Ford Motor Company Employee Development and Training Program (EDTP) illustrates the way these partnerships can work. It is an extensive project and, as such, has become the model on which other union-management partnerships are based. The EDTP program addresses the needs of both active and laid-off UAW-represented Ford hourly employees. The programs are funded through company contributions and administered through the UAW–Ford Motor Company National Development and Training Center. The center's staff consists of company and union representatives as well as professionals in education, counseling, training, placement, and information processing and coordinates activities and on-site assistance to some eighty-five local committees throughout the country. Neither the national center nor the local committees provide educational or training services directly but, rather, serve as brokers and contract for services with local government as well as social and educational institutions.

Originally, large-scale plant closings led the EDTP to focus on services for dislocated workers. To meet this demand, the EDTP committee set up several Career Services and Reemployment and Assistance Centers throughout the country. When a plant shuts down, the employees can go to a center and receive services such as counseling, education, placement, and relocation assistance. The centers rely partly on the community funding agencies to share costs and turn to people within the community to deliver the services. For this purpose the center staff develops networks of professionals, community leaders, and educational and placement resources to assist the displaced workers (Goldberg 1985).

The EDPT has now expanded its scope and provides assistance to active employees in addition to the displaced. These projects focus on broad personal development and growth objectives rather than just job training. In the program's life/education planning component, employees are aided through group and individual guidance in assessing their personal strengths and weaknesses and in learning about various educational and developmental opportunities that are available to them.

The alternatives that are open to them are not limited to activities that are immediately related to their current jobs. They may choose to continue their basic education, refresh skills such as math, language, and communication, or complete their formal education. Through the center they can finish high school or sign up for the College/University Options Program, which is designed to make higher education and college or university degree programs accessible to active employees. Regional faculty teams help assess students' prior learning experiences and conduct counseling workshops and course instructions at plant sites or union halls (Pascoe and Collins 1985).

Business-Education Cooperation

In the past, alliances between industry and education have focused on economic development through the improvement of primary and secondary schools. Businesses have assisted schools through a variety of mechanisms to help them prepare students for meeting the skill demands of the workplace. The cooperative efforts have included work-education projects consisting of career education, student internships, adopt-a-school programs, and seminars and summer jobs programs for teachers (Zemke 1985).

Another focal point has been postsecondary education. Businesses have collaborated with vocational schools to implement technical training programs in local communities that provide companies with a pool of prospective employees who have skills critical to their businesses. The National Pilot Program addresses this same goal on a broad scale. It is a project sponsored by General Electric, the U.S. Department of Labor, and the Greater Cincinnati Industrial Training Corporation to produce and sell a series of technical training courses to vocational schools, community colleges, and businesses throughout the nation.

Recently the nature of business-education partnerships has expanded. The focus is no longer exclusively on encouraging companies to assist in the long-term improvement of public schools. Now the educational institutions approach businesses as customers and provide training on a contractual basis for companies' employees. Corporations, for example, frequently contract with educational institutions or other community organizations for remedial education and literacy courses. Because the needs of individuals who enter basic skills programs vary, the instruction usually is customized and often begins as a one-on-one tutorial. An example of such an arrangement is the nine-year-old basic skills training program at Planters Peanuts. The program is implemented through a cooperative consisting of the company, the union, and the State Department of Education, and the instruction is provided by the local school system to company employees on their own time. Likewise, the Basic Skills Enhancement Program (BSEP) offered by the UAW–Ford

Sharing the Challenge

Motor Company Employee Development and Training Center is another business-education partnership. The BSEP projects were developed collaboratively by Ford, the UAW, and local school districts and operate similar to the Planters Peanut program. The joint venture provides training through the local school districts in reading and math matched to the individual's needs.

Many companies contract with local universities and community colleges to provide various retraining classes. Ford Motors and General Motors have formed partnerships with the UAW to implement large-scale retraining efforts. Both of these union-management arrangements involve contracting with two-year and four-year colleges to provide counseling, skills assessment, and retraining for workers who are threatened with losing their jobs. Similarly, AT&T, in partnership with the Communications Workers of America, is establishing a career counseling and training institute that follows the models established by Ford and GM (Fields 1986).

Many other corporations cooperate with educational institutions on a smaller scale to retrain employees. IBM Corporation conducts programs in which manufacturing employees are retrained to become maintenance operators for automated systems. Although the program is run by an experienced IBM manager, the instruction is provided by a local community college. IBM also is engaged in several other cooperative ventures with community colleges and universities in retraining employees to become computer programmers. In some cases, the programs are set up so that the participants obtain associate degrees as a result of the retraining.

Innumerable examples of these business-education retraining partnerships exist, but opinions of the soundness of this approach to retraining vary. Donald Clark, president of the National Association for Industry-Education Cooperation (NAIEC) has expressed concern for the "fragmented" approach to such partnerships and has been quoted as saying that the "major problem today is the lack of focus in developing an ongoing, collaborative relationship between the school and industry" (Zemke 1985). Others express the concern that postsecondary education institutions simply are not prepared to play a major role in the retraining that is needed in the United States (Fields 1986). Some business leaders complain that traditional educational institutions are neither flexible nor practical enough to design retraining programs that fit business and industry

Summary and Implications

needs. University teachers are often viewed by industry leaders as too academic and theoretical. On the other hand, university professors often regard business leaders as short-sighted when they request specific, practical skills classes at the expense of theory and deeper levels of analyses.

Representing a different point of view, Robert Kopecek, co-editor of *Customized Job Training for Business and Industry*, has argued that the local community college is the most cost-effective provider of training programs for the private sector. Ron Zemke, senior editor of *Training Magazine*, also argued that "If an organization has 5,000 or fewer employees, and is any but the high, high, high tech business, it can't find a better, cheaper training resource than the local community college." Zemke did not take a strong position with regard to this debate but noted that "cooperation" between educational institutions and business no longer emphasizes economic development through improving the public schools. Universities and public schools now view businesses and industries as potential "markets" for their services rather than "partners" (Zemke 1985).

The debate over the appropriate relationship between business and educational institutions will undoubtedly continue. Given the potential magnitude of the skill obsolescence problem facing this nation, partnerships will be mandatory for averting a crisis.

Summary and Implications

American businesses are committed to providing training to their employees. Even though many companies have struggled through hard times over the last few years, their training budgets remain large. That training is not evenly distributed throughout the workforce, however: Managers and professionals are still the most likely to receive formal training. Because skill obsolescence is not limited to the white-collar professions, training opportunities should be more evenly distributed across occupations.

Although the general commitment to training is strong in corporate America, specific retraining remains a low priority. Companies still prefer to hire new employees rather than retrain existing employees as positions open up. Only when businesses experience problems in finding people to hire for their vacant positions are they likely to assign retraining higher priority.

A major barrier to large-scale retraining is the high incidence of illiteracy and the lack of adequate basic skills in employees. Growing numbers of companies face this problem as they attempt to modernize their technologies and procedures. Because employees must read and write in order to be trainable, remedial education is becoming an important element in retraining.

Because the training needs are so great and so urgent, the private sector is collaborating with labor unions and the public sector in training and retraining initiatives. However, if these joint endeavors are to succeed in warding off the skill obsolescence threat, private businesses must be stronger partners and take more initiative in retraining their own employees.

Finally, educational institutions and businesses must come together to form focused and effective partnerships. Although academics and businesspeople often fail to speak the same language, the time has come for both to overcome differences and coordinate their efforts. Economic development, business survival, and healthy levels of employment depend on their cooperation.

References

Carnevale, A. P. 1986. "The Learning Enterprise." *Training and Development Journal* (January).

Fields, C. M. 1986. "Need to Retrain People in Changing Fields Confronts Colleges with Creative Challenge." *Chronicle of Higher Education* (September 17).

Goldberg, M. 1985. "UAW–Ford Employee Development and Training Program: Overview of Operations and Structure." *Labor Law Journal* (August).

Gordon, J. 1987. "Where the Training Goes." *Training: The Magazine of Human Resources Development* (October).

Hodgkinson, H. L. 1986. *Future Search: A Look at the Present.* NEA Tec. Rep. Washington, D.C.: National Education Association, Professional and Organizational Development/Office of Planning.

Lee, C. 1986. "Literacy Training: Hidden Need." *Training: The Magazine of Human Resources Development* (September).

———. 1987. "Where the Training Dollars Go." *Training: The Magazine of Human Resources Development* (October).

McClintock, R. H. 1984. "High-Tech Future of Business Requires Advanced Schedule of Worker Retraining." *AMA Forum* (November).

References

Pascoe, T. J., and R. J. Collins. 1985. "UAW–Ford Employee Development and Training Program: Overview of Operations and Structure." *Labor Law Journal* (August).

Ross, I. 1986. "Managing Corporations Take." *Fortune* (September).

Secretary of Labor's Task Force on Economic Adjustment and Worker Dislocation. 1986 *Economic Adjustment and Worker Dislocation in a Competitive Society.* Tec. Rep. (December).

Zemke, R. 1985. "Industry-Education Cooperation: Old Phrase with a Strange New Meaning." *Training: The Magazine of Human Resources Development* (July).

CHAPTER FOUR

Developing a Strategic Plan: *Linking Retraining to Corporate Goals*

AS CORPORATIONS reshape their futures through acquisitions, mergers, new products, and new technologies, they also reshape corporate programs, functions, and resources. Nevertheless, they often neglect to address how to redirect people to perform the new roles created by the changes (Rosow and Zager 1985). Frequently this neglect results in inefficiencies if not failures in implementing the changes. People who do not have the right skills cannot do their jobs, so that the entire company is likely to suffer from poor human resource planning.

Why Link Training to Long-Range Strategic Plans?

According to Leonard Nadler and Garland Wiggs (1986), managers must engage in three separate yet interdependent types of planning:

1. **Strategic planning**: the process of determining what business the organization should be in and identifying the financial, physical, and human resources that will be needed in the future;
2. **Long-range planning**: the process of developing a blueprint for achieving the goals established in the strategic plan;
3. **Functional planning**: the process of outlining specific tasks to be performed and the time frame for implementing the organizational goals.

According to these experts, solid planning has always been necessary for business growth but is crucial to business survival in turbulent times. Accordingly, U.S. corporations need to plan for their long-term personnel needs in order to prevent critical skill shortages in the future. These plans, moreover, must be tied to the company's overall strategy for the future. A key component of a sound strategic plan is a description of the hiring and training that is crucial to implementing the overall corporate strategy. This type of human resource planning ensures that the company will have enough people with the right skills at the right time to fill the company's needs.

If this goal is to be accomplished, planners need to know how to get input from the right people and how to distinguish long-term from short-term human resource plans. They must learn to project skill requirements, inventory employees' current skills, check for predictable misalignments, and perform cost/benefit comparisons of the potential ways to prevent skill shortages.

Soliciting Input from the Top

If hiring and training strategies are to be linked to the company's vision of its future, the highest-level decision makers in the company should help with development. Too often those responsible for human resources make plans that assume the status quo and take a "business as usual" approach while top-level corporate officers prepare for major changes in the direction and operation of the company.

If such a scenario is to be avoided, the company should construct a mechanism for establishing communication between the two groups. This can be accomplished in a variety of ways. Perhaps the vice president for training could serve as a member of the strategic planning team. Although this practice is unusual within corporate America, a few companies do use this approach. At Caterpillar the manager of technical education is also a member of the strategy development team. Likewise, Travelers Insurance, a company that relies heavily on data-processing technology, includes the vice president for training on the corporate strategy planning committee. Some companies take a reverse approach to creating this line of communication. These companies have members of the strategy team sit on the training committees. At Motorola the CEO is a member of the committee that sets the policy for technical training (Rosow and Zager 1985).

Although the company's strategic plan will not spell out the specifics of the training programs to be developed, it should direct the assessment of the company's future skill needs. Training plans are then based on these projections. Training then becomes a central part of all corporate activities, for the implementation of business strategy depends on it. As Nadler and Wiggs (1986) argue, human resource development staff can no longer assess performance simply by counting the number of programs offered or the number of participants trained in a year. As they put it, "HRD planning today must reflect the constantly evolving and fluid nature of the organization's business as it strives to cope with competition as well as changes in psychology, markets, and its products or service mix."

Distinguishing Long-Term from Short-Term Personnel Plans

Pictures of the future are imprecise, but a good business plan requires long-range analyses and forecasts. Just as companies predict future markets and consumer values, they also should envision what their human resource needs are likely to be in five to ten years. These projections may not be as detailed or as accurate as six-month or one-year forecasts, yet they provide a framework for making strategy as well as operational decisions. As unforeseen events take place, the framework can be adjusted.

Most companies make human resource projections in the course of normal business planning, but these projections are usually made for relatively short periods of time, such as six months to a year. The rationale for long-range planning is that some policy decisions that a company makes today will affect the availability of labor far into the future. For example, a company's policy on early retirement affects the composition of the workforce ten years down the road. Hiring and training policies also affect whether employees have the skills that will be critical to the success of the business in the next decade.

Even when planners use a long time frame to make human resource projections, they frequently base them on assumptions from the past and the present that will not hold in the future. Replacement planning, for example, identifies people who could step into

Distinguishing Long-Term from Short-Term Personnel Plans

the company's key positions in the future. Thus, company executives might identify two or three people who could take over if the general manager were killed in a plane crash. Then they would look at the type of experience and training that would prepare these people for the general manager's role. This kind of planning is sufficient for a company with a future that looks substantially like its present, but few companies actually fit that description. Companies that make that assumption are often dangerously complacent: They do not take into account new key positions that might be developed, nor do they consider possible changes in the nature of the existing key positions.

Falling into a similar trap are techniques such as statistical forecasting models premised on how the organization is presently staffed and how it has been staffed in the past. Once again, the underlying assumption is that the company will not change. If the plan is to be useful, however, it must account for trends that might affect the company's future. Planners should analyze how the company's direction and strategy are likely to be affected by external events such as innovations in technology, shifts in the economy, government regulations, and changes in social values (Frantzreb 1981). As consumers' needs change, companies adjust the products that they offer. For example, when offices turned from typewriters to computers, a leading office equipment manufacturer made a similar change in the emphasis in its products. This change in product importance affected the salesforce and service representatives, who could not rely on the same body of knowledge to sell computers that they used to sell typewriters.

In the same way, developments in technologies affect how goods are made. As these products and processes change, the skills that are critical to the employer also shift. One example of this is the replacement of the standardized mass culture of the industrial era by societies that value diversity and individuality. To a great extent, new technologies have supported this diversification: Flexible manufacturing systems have enabled us to move beyond mass production into high tech customization. In fact, over the next decade programmable robots are likely to make it possible to manufacture one of a kind products. As more programmable robots are introduced into factories, the skills that employees need to work with the robots will change. Human resource planners must consider industrial trends outside of the company as they create forecasts. As values change, products change. As products change, processes change. As processes change, skill requirements change. The useful strategic human resource plan will equip companies to anticipate rather than react to at least some of the changes in their businesses precipitated by these trends.

Still another problem with current methods for projecting human resource requirements is that usually such forecasts are limited to predicting the number of people that will be needed within broad occupations or job classifications. The projections do not analyze the types of skills required to do the job, even though we are currently witnessing a dramatic and quick shift in the essential expertise for many occupations. The field of engineering serves as a case in point. Most occupational analysts claim that the demand for engineers is growing, but that fact alone does not really help trainers and educators. The important information for planning educational and training programs concerns the backgrounds and capabilities that engineers need to work with increasingly sophisticated technologies. In their book *Human Resource Implications of Robotics*, Hunt and Hunt (1983) argue that engineers are not receiving the right education for maintaining and supporting robotics technology once installed. They assert that American universities are still turning out engineering specialists rather than generalists who understand the potential of robotics. Training and education planners need to know not only how many engineers employers will need but what those engineers will be required to do. Therefore, these "numbers" projections are not useful for planning educational and training programs.

Although there is no formula for making accurate human resource forecasts, we can clearly identify some of the factors that must be considered. First, planners can conduct some type of demand forecasting, including how many and what kinds of people the company will need. Second, they should carry out an investigation of the current supply. This analysis would focus on how many current employees will be available in the future and the extent to which those employees possess the skills identified in the demand analysis. The third step is to compare the projected demand for skills with the predicted supply. The size of the discrepancy between the two will indicate the company's long-term risk of suffering a shortage of critical skills. In assessing the supply, the company should look at its own current workforce as well as the projections for the overall labor force for the upcoming years. If the company will not have the skills it needs based on the workers it already employs, it must examine whether it is likely to be able to hire people with the appropriate capabilities. There is already a labor and critical skill scarcity in the United States that is creating hiring problems for many companies. These shortages will probably grow over the next decade.

Assessing Demand: Projecting Skill Requirements

The first step in strategic human resource planning is to project the company's future skill requirements. To do this effectively, the planners need input from key people throughout the company. These critical people can help the planners put together an inventory of expected jobs.

Job Analysis

Once the planners know the expected array of jobs they can perform job analyses. A complete analysis includes examining each position for

> Content
> Processes
> On-the-job hazards/working conditions
> Physical requirements
> Education, knowledge, and skill-level requirements
> Experience needed

Planners must pay special attention to activities that can be performed by only a limited number of people, such as jobs that are sex, age, education, or experience specific. The jobs should be examined closely to see if the restrictions are really necessary. For example, planners can look at whether experience can be substituted for education and vice versa. Likewise, they can examine whether on-the-job training can substitute for education. Of course, the less restrictive the job requirements, the less vulnerable the company is to labor shortages. Eliminating roles that are sex specific or age specific is not only a way of avoiding shortages in workers but also a means of complying with federal discrimination statutes.

Skills and Knowledge Analysis

The most important part of job analysis is identifying the skills and knowledge necessary for performance. Several skill classification systems are available for the analysis. As planners choose a system or develop their own system, they should be sure to address several skill categories, including

> Cognitive skills
> Technical skills
> Work-content skills
> Interpersonal skills
> Self-management skills

Some of the classification systems also include a class that is more attitudinal than skill-oriented. Commitment to task completion or interest in one's work might fall into this category. Once the skill categories are identified, each grouping should be broken down into specific subdivisions. For instance, the cognitive skills category could be broken down into different types of reasoning. The classifications might include analytic reasoning, such as examining and evaluating data, and synthetic reasoning, such as creating new approaches to problems and developing systems. In addition, the level of competency for each skill classification must be addressed.

It is crucial that the analyses take into consideration both the technical and social aspects of the job—an approach that often is referred to as sociotechnical analyses. The assessment should consider skills that will be required to use the tools and techniques for accomplishing the tasks. Additionally, the appraisal should also project the aptitudes and attitudes required to work within the social system. The social system includes factors such as how work is divided and coordinated and how people must relate to each other to get the job done.

As a result of long-range planning, a medium-sized midwestern bank with several branches decided to distinguish itself from other banks in the region through a strategy that made high-quality personal services its highest priority. As an outgrowth of this plan, the company decided to reorganize many departments, including customer services, over an eighteen-month time period. It decided to assign customer service employees to multiskilled work teams. Each team would be qualified to handle all of the inquiries and complaints for all the products and services that the bank offered. In addition, the teams would be responsible for designing customer relations activities for the geographic area in which their branch was located. The company conducted a skills analysis to find out what individuals would need to be able to do in order for these teams to operate effectively. They concluded that all employees would need to understand the technical information about the bank's many services and would need a set of skills pertaining to working with a team. They would need group process and group problem-solving skills and would need to be able to develop team goals and to coordinate their activities. This assessment gave the bank a foundation for building its transitional training program. The driving force behind this program was the bank president, who believed that the bank should actively pursue its change strategy rather than wait to react when crises developed.

In short, skills analyses must be linked to a company's strategic and long-range plans and should be based on: trends within an industry, within the company, and within occupations. The forecasts should be made as far in advance as possible to allow lead time for setting up programs to meet the skill needs.

Assessing Supply: Identifying Employees' Skills

After planners project the occupational and skill demands, their next step is to develop a picture of the probable supply of those skills, which involves predicting how many employees will be available in the various occupational and skill categories after allowing for events such as turnover, retirement, and promotion. Companies use a variety of methods for calculating the likely supply of people. One rather imprecise method is to analyze the skills that are required to perform the current jobs within the company and then to make a rough count of the numbers of people in each job category. The result is a rough estimate of the skill supply.

A better approach is to inventory the employees' individual skills, talents, and qualifications. Some companies use these inventories from employees and their managers to create job skills banks that they use for their projections of skill supply. The banks also are useful for identifying employees with the experiences and skills needed for special projects and for matching employees with available jobs. First, they develop a system (often computerized) for coding a wide variety of skills and experiences. Next, they construct instructions that explain the classification system to the employees. With assistance from their managers, individuals can then develop their own skill profiles. These profiles usually contain facts pertaining to skills, work experiences, education, and achievements. To increase the precision of the input, some systems have a method for entering proficiency levels into the system. Assuming that the data entered are accurate, the more precise the classification system, the more useful for the analysis of supply.

A large multinational corporation that is innovative in many of its personnel activities has developed a skill-planning model that uses personal computers for the information input. Managers are required to update employee facts in the system so that the personnel resource planning staff can use the data for human resource needs assessments.

The company is committed to providing employment security to all of its thousands of employees. This commitment can be honored only through careful human resource planning and heavy investment in training. Retraining is almost "business as usual" for this corporation. The company has not laid off any employees for years, and in return, employees are almost fiercely loyal to the company. Careful planning and strong commitments can pay off for the entire corporation and especially for the people who work for it.

Assessing and projecting a company's supply of skills is not an easy task. Yet every company that wants to avoid the possibility of having too many people with the wrong kind of competencies and too few with the right abilities must meet the challenge. This proactive approach has long-term payoffs for the company, but immediate benefits also come from the assessment. Indeed, sound personnel decisions depend on accurate and current information about employees' qualifications, education, skills, and experiences. A thorough skills inventory should become an invaluable aid to personnel.

Checking for Imbalances

Once a company projects its skills supply and demand, planners can determine the degree to which the two will be balanced. Many companies find that they have an existing imbalance that will worsen over time. They are pressed to develop a strategy for solving the immediate problem as well as averting the potential plight. Of course, retraining is not the only solution to a projected skill misalignment. Table 4–1 illustrates the range of possible solutions. Another option is to devise strategies that attract and retain key employees who have the critical skills. For instance, a company may raise pay scales or add incentives for jobs that are likely to be hard to fill. Alternatively, companies could try more radical approaches, such as moving employees from one operation where their skills are no longer needed to other plants or offices that could use them. Some companies have actually moved operations from one geographic area to another in order to have a pool of workers with appropriate qualifications. Some other options that might be considered include redefining priorities so that some work can be eliminated or contracting with another company to do work.

Although companies address the problem in many ways, the most popular approach is often referred to as "fire and hire." Firms wait until their workers' skills have become obsolete, fire them, and hire new employees to do the jobs. Not only does this practice exert a heavy toll on the people who are dismissed, but it is not likely to be viable for long because of the impending nationwide labor shortage. Moreover, firing and hiring may not be any less expensive than

Table 4–1: Options for Addressing Skill Imbalances

Retrain
Attract and retain employees with critical skills
Move employees to another site
Move company operations to an area with a qualified labor pool
Eliminate some work
Fire and hire

retraining existing employees to meet the company's skill needs, even though companies often assume that firing and hiring is the least costly solution to their skill needs. There is no perfect solution to the problem of fixing or preventing skill imbalances. All options have some drawbacks. The problem must be addressed, however, or companies will flounder. Skill imbalances affect the bottom line and cannot be ignored. If a company uncovers an existing or a projected skill imbalance, the executives should consider all angles of the available options and choose one that effectively fits their circumstances.

Cost/Benefit Comparisons

The popular practice of firing and hiring is often assumed to be a solution to skill imbalances that is economically superior to other options such as retraining existing employees. This assumption is frequently incorrect even if only quantifiable costs are taken into account. Sometimes companies err by figuring the costs of training, rejecting this option as too costly, and not assessing the expense of firing and hiring. There is a quantifiable dollar value associated with firing an individual. The Work in America Institute has estimated that the cost of dismissing any semiskilled employee is approximately $8,900 (Rosow and Zager 1987). This figure includes such expenses as severance, unemployment compensation, and loss of production value. In addition, the less quantifiable yet significant costs in firing include the loss of loyal employees who have a knowledge and experience base with the company. Moreover, if large numbers of people are dismissed due to changing skill requirements, those employees who remain may suffer a drop in morale and a fear of anything new. Resistance to change can grow because employees may suspect that modern technologies and streamlined procedures could cost them their jobs. The resulting drop in productivity can exact a tremendous price. When a company identifies a potential imbalance in the supply and demand of skills, planners should perform a thorough cost accounting before choosing a method for eliminating the problem.

The Work in America Institute has recommended a method for

comparing the costs of retraining to firing and hiring (Rosow and Zager 1985). The first step is to identify the skills required for the positions or occupations with the projected undersupply of workers. Next, analysts figure what it would cost to train people who have either very low-level skills or none of the skills required for these jobs; this analysis should be done by breaking the training into components. If the job requires knowledge of three computer languages, the ability to work with two different types of computer hardware, and the ability to solve problems in a group, costs should be figured for at least six training components. It may be necessary to break these six components into even smaller units to accurately estimate expenses. Group problem solving, for example, includes a number of skills, such as knowledge of the mechanics of reaching consensus, communication abilities, and proficiency in organizing tasks. These capabilities could be addressed through one class or several separate modules.

This first set of estimates can serve as a baseline for figuring actual costs. If accurate, these base estimates mark the upper limit for project expenditures. Of course, in most cases the actual outlays fall well below this upper limit because the people who are selected for the program are likely to meet some of the qualifications. Rarely are jobs within a company completely unique with skills that are entirely exclusive to one position; the qualifications for almost any job are likely to overlap with the requirements for other jobs.

The next step is to select the job categories within the company from which trainees could be chosen. The competencies required for these positions should be stacked up against the prerequisites needed for the undersupplied positions. This analysis should focus on the overlap in the job categories. After making that comparison, planners can pinpoint the training that would be necessary to move employees from each of the jobs under consideration into the new positions. In many cases, the company considers several job categories for the selection of candidates. Analysts should construct a total cost matrix that outlines the probable expense of retraining people from each job category. People who are performing jobs that have some abilities that overlap with the new job will require less training than will workers in jobs with little overlap. In general, the lower the training requirements, the lower the cost of the program. For example, in the case of training to increase the supply of word processor operators, people who know how to type are cheaper to train than are people without keyboard skills.

Once the cost matrix for retraining has been constructed, analysts must figure the expenses associated with hiring a new employee who is already fully trained. Securing new employees usually requires outlays for staffing recruiters and for administering recruitment and selection. Companies also must provide orientation and some training for new employees because in general, they do not have all of the knowledge needed to merely step in and perform their jobs.

Two other sets of costs should also figure into the comparison. Strategists should figure the price of firing employees, and calculations would include things like severance pay, counseling, and outplacement assistance. Finally, because some skills required for the undersupplied jobs are likely to be scarce even outside of the company, the cost of not being able to fill the position should be calculated.

After identifying all of these figures, planners can compare the costs of retraining various groups of people to the costs of firing and hiring to see which alternative is most cost efficient. Of course, those who are making these comparisons should remember that there are additional, less quantifiable penalties associated with firing, such as lowered morale and productivity among remaining employees. Planners have to decide how to weigh these less measurable but nevertheless real losses into the choice of alternatives.

A somewhat complicated yet often cost-effective approach to handling a skill imbalance through retraining is to select candidates who already meet some of the qualifications for the new positions regardless of whether they come from jobs that are oversupplied. As they vacate jobs, their previous positions could be available to the people who are in the oversupply job categories. This approach is less direct in solving the imbalance problem than merely selecting people from job categories with shrinking demand. In the long run it may be more effective and less expensive than the more direct approach, however, because the most highly qualified people rather than the most vulnerable would be selected for the training program. This method capitalizes on making the best match of people with opportunities.

Summary and Implications

As companies change their strategies, processes, and products, they must ensure that their workers can perform the new roles created by those changes. The development of long-term human resource plans therefore must be tied to the company's strategic plan.

A useful human resource plan examines whether there will be a balance between the skills available in the workforce and the skills required for a particular array of jobs. If the assessment uncovers a probable imbalance, the company must find a way to prevent problems. This involves comparing the costs and benefits of retraining to the costs and benefits of other alternatives. Before making these comparisons, planners decide how much intangibles such as morale and loyalty weigh in the process of choosing solutions.

References

Frantzreb, R. B. 1981. "Human Resource Planning: Forecasting Manpower Needs." *Personnel Journal* (November).

Hunt, H. A., and T. Hunt. 1983. *Human Resource Implications of Robotics*. Kalamazoo, Mich.: W. E. Upjohn Institute for Employment Research.

Nadler, L., and G. D. Wiggs. 1986. *Managing Human Resource Development*. San Francisco: Jossey-Bass, p. 213.

Rosow, J. M., and R. Zager. 1987. *Training for New Technology: Part I, Linking Training Strategy to Corporate Strategy*. Scarsdale, N.Y.: Work in America Policy Study Institute, p. 13.

———. 1987. *Training for New Technology: Part IV, The Continuous Learning/Employment Security Connection*. Scarsdale, N.Y.: Work in America Policy Study Institute.

CHAPTER 5

Planning and Administering the Program:
Who Does What and When?

As with all training programs, the success of retraining is determined by careful planning. Training projects that are launched without careful attention to design details result in reduced effectiveness if not complete disaster, but sound and effective retraining programs evolve from the coordinated efforts of a team of people who work with the program from start to finish. The members of this team plan, implement, and evaluate the entire training program, monitor the project as it is executed, and, on its completion, gauge whether the project achieved its goals. Such planning is critical to retraining because the intended results of such programs are highly specific and extremely important to both the organization and the trainees themselves. Table 5–1 illustrates the three stages in the retraining process and the purpose of each stage.

Forming the Retraining Program Team

Once decision makers have decided to initiate a retraining program, they must define the roles of those who will be responsible for the process. First, they should designate the department within the company that will oversee the project and the individuals who should work with the department. Of course, the size of the company and the nature and scope of the program influences who should participate. Programs that require trainees to make a major career transition and acquire entirely new skills must involve more de-

Table 5–1: Stages in a Retraining Program

Planning, design, and development

To produce a plan for the retraining program that defines
    Rationale for the program
    Roles and responsibilities
    Selection, training, and placement details

To produce a curriculum plan that defines
    Overall objectives of training
    Courses and training modules to be delivered
    Delivery methods

Implementation

To carry out the retraining plan by
    Selecting trainees and arranging for their placement
    Delivering the training

Evaluation

To determine whether the program achieved its goal by
    Evaluating whether immediate training goals were met
    Assessing whether the program met the business goals
    Analyzing the long-term impact of retraining

partments within the company than programs of more limited scope. Sometimes small-scale training needs can be handled through the company's traditional training programs, whereas larger needs may require special efforts. These special programs will be most successful if planned and administered through the coordinated activities of several departments within the company. Likely candidates for the retraining team include the personnel, education, and communications groups, as well as the departments to which the trainees will be assigned after they complete the program. Again, the responsibilities and the degree of involvement of each of these groups will vary according to the particulars of the specific venture. Whatever the nature of the program, however, each of these areas has certain core duties and tasks. Every department that participates in the program should designate someone to serve on the retraining program team. In addition, the team should be headed by a program manager who is responsible for overseeing the entire operation.

Planning and Administering the Program

Team Members' Responsibilities

Table 5–2 summarizes the roles of team members from each of the three major groups. All team members are responsible for ensuring that their respective departments fulfill their responsibilities.

Education. The education team member is responsible for providing input and advising on any issues that pertain to curriculum or to instruction. In addition, this person instructs other team members about general retraining program issues such as how to design and deliver training. In many cases, an individual from the education department is the best qualified to assume the role of program manager because education and training are the heart of the program. In any event, education staff members should work closely with whoever takes on the responsibilities of program management. The education department's primary contributions include verifying that training is an appropriate solution to a skill imbalance

Table 5–2: Roles and Responsibilities of Committee Members

Education	Personnel	Communications
Clarify education issues	Assist with selection and placement process	Help analyze the effect of the program on morale
Advise on program design and delivery	Review program materials	Advise on creating positive climate for retraining
Assist or conduct skills assessment	Assess effect of program on human resource policy	Determine how program will be advertised internally
Verify that training will meet the business goals	Ensure that program conforms to personnel policies	Determine how program will be advertised externally
Assist with selection of training provider	Track career progress of program graduates	Advise managers on how to discuss the program with employees

problem, assisting with the assessment of precise skill needs, and determining the optimal system for the delivery of the training.

Personnel. The primary responsibility of the personnel team member is to keep the program manager informed concerning how personnel policies and practices will either affect or be affected by the project. Personnel's contribution is especially important in assisting with the selection and placement of trainees, reviewing program materials, and determining how the program affects any other human resource policies throughout the company.

Personnel also plays a major role in monitoring the career progress of the trainees once they complete the program. This is especially important in large companies where employees frequently move from one department to another or from one location to another. The personnel staff members need to set up a system to track the graduates of the program so that the company can evaluate the long-term effectiveness of the retraining.

Communications. The communications staff is responsible for all of the publicity needs of the program. Their efforts can encourage employee acceptance of the retraining project. Sometimes the development of a retraining program triggers anxiety throughout the company because the employees view it as a sign of change. Because most of us are, at best, ambivalent about change and, at worst, terrified of how change will affect us, the climate in which the retraining program is established can have a major effect on morale, and these effects often extend beyond the groups that are directly involved in the retraining. The communications people, therefore, along with others on the planning team, should carefully analyze the possible effect of the program on morale and climate within the entire company.

Labor Union. Many companies establish partnerships with labor unions for planning and executing retraining programs. Either the president of the local union or one or more designated representatives should serve on the retraining team to provide input and advise on all issues from the standpoint of their membership. Because a large number, if not all, of the trainees probably will come from their ranks, the union team members can provide input on how the various components of the program will affect the trainees.

Program Manager. The retraining program manager plays the most significant part in determining the program's success because this person coordinates the entire retraining process. The program manager oversees the planning, development, and implementation of the project and serves as liaison among all those involved in the undertaking. Therefore, one of the first and most crucial tasks for the company's decision makers is to define the role of the program manager and to select an individual to fill that position. Because the program manager is vital for providing coordination and continuity for the program, the person should fill this role from the beginning to the end of the program. When this role is switched from one person to another before the project is completed, not only is continuity lost but trainees who form close ties with this individual feel less secure. Most often the program manager should originate from the education area or the area in which the trainees will be placed after completing the training. In cases where retraining programs are administered through union-management partnerships, co-program managers are appropriate, but if two people serve this function, they must clarify from the beginning their individual responsibilities and authority.

The demands of the program manager's job require an individual who can effectively interact with management, negotiate and coordinate program activities, creatively solve problems, and be sensitive to trainees' needs. The manager's responsibilities do not end until the training is completed and the trainees have begun their new jobs. In general, the program manager's responsibilities include conducting the retraining committee meetings, coordinating between the program personnel and upper-level management, coordinating and negotiating decisions made as the program is planned, overseeing the implementation of the program, and organizing the assessment of the program on its completion.

Examples of Team Composition. Companies vary in their choices of who should serve on the retraining teams and task forces. Xerox Corporation put together a task force to design, monitor, and oversee a critical skills retraining program for the Retrographics

Business Group (RBG) located in Rochester, New York. The program focused on computer and microprocessor theory and applications including both hardware and software and prepared employees to meet the company's high tech skill needs. The task force for this retraining program was composed of representatives from the managers from RBG's human resource staff, managers from RBG, managers from several divisions of Xerox that would employ the program's graduates, and representatives from the Rochester Institute of Technology (Morano and Leonardi 1987).

At Packard Electric, training and retraining falls under the umbrella of a union-management Quality of Worklife (QWL) program. Manufacturing supervisors, engineering supervisors, hourly operators, QWL staff members, union representatives, and human resource consultants normally comprise the training design teams for their many retraining endeavors (Hemmens 1987).

At a much smaller service firm, a retraining team was established to design and oversee a secretarial program. The team was composed of the personnel and training manager and her only staff member, the one communications director employed by the company, the assistant to the general manager, and the Office Systems department chair from the local community college.

The retraining task forces and teams that companies assemble are diverse. Large corporations with well-established and ongoing union-management quality of work life programs are likely to have clearly defined mechanisms for deciding who to include on the retraining team. At the other end of the continuum are the smaller companies with less formal policies and procedures for initiating new programs. Each company, and frequently each program, is unique in its needs for the composition of the retraining team.

Developing the Program Plan

Once the retraining team is in place, the program manager distributes the background materials so that committee members can become familiar with the rationale and objectives for the project. Additionally, the team also studies similar retraining efforts that have been conducted either within the company or by other establishments. Once the team members have studied the background data, they can then begin to develop the retraining program plan.

This program plan is the blueprint for the entire retraining project and, as such, is an important document. It should contain detailed descriptions of each of the steps in the entire retraining process. For instance, the plan should outline the business rationale, program objectives, and roles and responsibilities of each team member. It also should present the step-by-step procedures for designing, implementing, and evaluating the overall operation. All of the departments and areas represented on the retraining program team should jointly produce this blueprint. Even though the general scheme was probably sketched out by the managers who initiated the program, the team members will have to fill in the details, and this probably will require them to negotiate their duties and responsibilities. In order to avoid confusion, they should document, in the plan, commitments that they make through these negotiations.

Business Rationale Statement

The first element of the program plan is a rationale statement that provides an overview of the business conditions that created a skill imbalance and describes the nature of the problem. In addition, it recounts the options that the company's decision makers considered as possible solutions to the imbalance and, finally, describes how and why the company chose retraining instead of other options for dealing with the skill imbalance dilemma.

Program Goals and Objectives

The second element of the program plan is a synopsis of the project's goals and objectives. Because the mission of any retraining program is to fulfill an identified business need, this element should flow directly from the rationale statement. The business rationale might state that the strategic manpower projections revealed a demand for 100 additional computer programmers over the next two years. If a cost/benefit analysis pointed to the conclusion that at least half of those programmers should be developed internally, the specific program objectives might be (1) to prevent a shortage of programmers by training fifty people to assume entry-level computer programmer responsibilities and (2) to place those people in jobs at their current location within a year.

Developing the Program Plan

Roles and Responsibilities

The third element of the plan is a definition of the retraining program team's responsibilities with special emphasis on the role of the retraining program manager. In order for the team to function effectively, all members need guidelines delineating the scope of their authority. For example, will the team make all of the program decisions, or will it draft a proposal to present to upper management, who will retain the final authority? If the team members are to be in charge of making some decisions, they need to know who must be kept informed of their plans. Likewise, they need clarification on when, how, and to whom they report program progress. Finally, in almost any program, upper management reserves the right to withdraw authority from the team under some circumstances. These conditions must be clearly defined from the outset.

Skills Required

The most crucial element of the program plan is the analysis of the skills that the trainees must have mastered by the time they complete the program. Of course, portions of this analysis should have been performed when the decision makers were determining whether a retraining program was needed. Nevertheless, a more thorough study is in order as the committee constructs a program plan that builds on the previous one.

The team committee should rely on an expert in skills and needs assessment procedures to perform this task. Of course, if the analysis is to be done right, the expert works closely with people in the areas where the trainees will be placed on completing the program. Together, they examine the jobs to be performed looking for the following three types of skills:

1. *Technical skills:* skills that involve the mastery of a particular vocabulary, procedure, or subject matter, such as typing or computer programming;
2. *Self-management skills:* skills that allow individuals to adapt appropriately to a specific work environment (time management, self-reliance);
3. *Functional skills:* basic skills required to deal with data, people, or things; skills not tied to knowledge of specific procedures and

thus transferable across jobs (problem solving, analyzing, persuading, coordinating).

All too often, the skills analysis that planners perform is much too limited in scope. One of the most common errors that analysts make when identifying skills is to focus exclusively on the technical or work-content skills and to exclude the other two skill categories. If the trainees are to succeed in their new roles after they have completed the program, they must not only be technically competent but also be able to adjust to the new work environment. In order to identify all of the employee's needed abilities, the analysis should consider characteristics of the job such as the division of labor, the coordination of roles, the flow of information and materials, as well as any other components of the work environment that might affect job performance (Pava 1983).

The new roles often are fundamentally different from the old and require learning not only new technical skills but an unfamiliar approach to work. Take, for example, a retraining program with the objective of teaching statistical process control to quality inspectors. Previously the inspectors' tasks may have involved identifying and throwing out work that did not meet specifications, but the new tasks consist of identifying the variables in the production process that account for the defects in the product. Not only do the quality inspectors need to know statistical procedures for pinpointing the causes of defects, but they must learn to cooperate with other people involved in the production process. Because they are very dependent on others for the information that allows them to do their jobs, the new roles require stronger interpersonal and team skills. As the quality inspectors retrain, they must learn to view themselves as problem solvers rather than as watchdogs, which means that they need to change their relationships with others from adversarial to cooperative. Thus, a complete skills analysis extends to interpersonal skills and attitudes in addition to technical skills.

A second way in which analysts often mistakenly limit their skills analysis is to study only entry-level skill requirements. This approach ignores skills that would allow for career growth and advancement. Thus, the trainees find themselves in dead-end jobs once again because they are not adequately prepared for competing with others who are pursuing the same career path. If this situation is to be avoided, program planners need to study several levels within the career path to determine the skill foundation that trainees will need for advancement. Of course, most retraining programs cannot provide instruction in all the higher-level skills that the trainees eventually will need. Nevertheless, graduates of the retraining program should be equipped with the fundamentals on which a growth and development plan can be built.

Once the committee is satisfied that the skills analysis is complete, they can refine their program objectives. For example, suppose that the program goal is to prepare twenty-five people to fill entry-level secretarial positions. The skills analysis indicates that secretarial positions require keyboard skills, familiarity with word processing, ability to organize and manage time, and a mastery of spelling and grammar. The program objectives are to graduate twenty-five people from the program who can demonstrate a designated performance level of each of these skills. The plan also indicates the type of evidence that the committee will use to verify that graduates actually possess designated skills after retraining. Operational details for the retraining endeavor cannot be worked out until objectives are clearly defined: The action plan must evolve from the objectives rather than vice versa.

Selection Process

One of the first and most basic steps in developing the action plan is to decide how to select the trainees. The committee members have to address several issues pertaining to selection. The first step, and one critical to the success of the program, is to determine whether the program is to be voluntary or involuntary. Although the business rationale and program goal often dictate that decision, committee members still must assess how overall objectives affect the targeted group of trainees. If the program goal is to upgrade a particular group of employees' skills so that they can continue to function in their existing jobs, then everyone within that group will be required to retrain. However, if the goal is to alleviate a skill shortage within the company through a retraining program, then participation can be voluntary. If the program is to solve a skill imbalance or prevent layoffs, however, establishing who should be retrained is more difficult. Whatever the circumstances, participation in the retraining program should be voluntary whenever possible because coercion almost always depresses motivation to learn and to adjust.

When participation in the program is voluntary, the next step is to establish the selection criteria, which requires careful review of the applicant's qualifications on entering the program. Some companies administer aptitude tests as one way to predict an applicant's possible success in the program. If aptitude tests are to be administered, the selection team should be careful to choose tests with proven validity. There must be concrete evidence that the test actually predicts success in the program and the profession. Some companies use aptitude tests as diagnostic tools. Applicants who are strong candidates in some respects but who do not score well on aptitude tests are given special remedial training so that they can succeed in future retraining programs.

In any case, committee members must learn the background and skills of each applicant because this information directly affects the types of courses that must be included in the curriculum and the level at which those courses must be taught. To some degree, the trainees' aptitudes, skills, and backgrounds influence the topics to be included. Therefore, to a limited degree, the program objectives can be achieved or at least facilitated through the selection process as well as through the training itself.

Suppose that the skills analysis indicates that on graduation, the trainees must be able to use a personal computer and write clear reports. The program planners might decide to choose people who already have strong keyboard skills and can write well, and then focus the training exclusively on the mechanics of using a personal computer. On the other hand, they could choose people who are likely to be displaced from their existing jobs regardless of their ability to write well and type. Thus, the training would need to address these skills along with the personal computer competencies. As a second example, suppose that the skills analyses indicate that job performance will require electromechanical skills that depend on a solid background in math. Program planners must decide whether to make the math background a criteria for selection or whether to include some basic math courses in the curriculum.

Likewise, if the job will require good communication skills such as proper grammar and spelling, will the participants be expected to possess those skills when entering, or will these subjects be taught in the program?

In general, as the number of courses increases, the time and budget required for the training expands. Furthermore, when trainees have lower competency levels in the skills addressed by the curriculum, a more detailed and lengthy instructional process is needed. In determining the criteria by which candidates are to be selected, the committee therefore must first look at the program's budget and time frame.

Finally, the team must determine which of the job qualifications are actually trainable. Suppose that the skills analysis indicates that strong interpersonal skills, such as the ability to develop rapport, are needed. The committee has to decide whether trainees can actually be taught to establish these connections with others. They should rely on the expertise of personnel or education specialists in making these judgments. Some characteristics may not be trainable within a reasonable time frame and budget, so that committee members may want to require trainees to be already skilled in those areas that cannot realistically be addressed within the constraints of the program. If the retraining program is to produce graduates who can be productive in the new jobs, all of the skills that are identified in the skills analyses should be addressed either through the selection process or through the curriculum.

By far the most effective strategy for determining selection criteria is, first, to make preliminary decisions about what can be included in the training curriculum and, then, to establish selection criteria that admit to the program persons who have the appropriate qualifications for succeeding within that curriculum. Nevertheless, sometimes the selection process is subject to constraints. For instance, the program may be limited to those who are most vulnerable to immediate job displacement. In some companies, the retraining may be further restricted to those who have the most seniority within the target group. Under these circumstances, selection probably will be based not merely on qualifications but rather by eligibility requirements. When these conditions prevail, planners should draw up a general profile of the eligible group that includes the educational background, experience, and skills that members are likely to have at the beginning of the program. The committee would compare that profile to a profile of the occupation trainees will be entering and design a curriculum to eliminate any discrepancies between the two.

Even if the selection is restricted to a target group, individuals who are eligible vary in their aptitudes, backgrounds, and skills, and selection criteria based on those factors can still be established. For example, if the new jobs require electromechanical skills that depend on a strong math background, program planners can determine the general math proficiency within the group targeted for training and select those individuals who have the strongest math backgrounds and aptitudes. If, however, everyone is to be retrained and is likely to be deficient in basic math skills, the committee members can adjust the curriculum to include some math courses.

Planners should keep in mind that if program eligibility is restricted to a narrow target group, the pool of applicants is likely to be less qualified than if the program is open to everyone in the company. Of course, the more qualified the applicants, the greater the probability that those who are chosen will succeed in the training program. Again, decision makers should not lose sight of the original business rationale for the retraining program. If the reason for initiating the project was to ensure that employees would not be displaced, then these selection decisions should be made within that framework.

After the committee establishes the selection criteria, it can then outline the selection process. The first step is to determine who nominates the candidates. In some cases, the committee may decide to advertise the program to employees and allow them to submit their own applications. An alternative is to ask managers to nominate their most qualified employees, a method that cuts down on the applicant screening time. The team needs to decide how to screen applicants. For example, if a large number of people apply to the program, will the team interview all applicants, or will some be eliminated through studying resumés and application forms? Will the final selection decision be based on one set of interviews, or will finalists be interviewed a second time? How many people will interview each applicant? The selection process decisions can be summarized as follows:

Developing the Program Plan

1. How many screening steps will be needed?
2. Who will conduct the screening?
3. How will the applicants' qualifications be measured?
4. Who will make the final decisions?

Managers from the areas in which program graduates will be placed should definitely be involved in the selection process. Ideally, these managers not only help select candidates but make job commitments to those who are selected.

Placement Process

If job commitments cannot be made to specific individuals as they are selected for the retraining program, the committee should try to obtain assurances from managers to accept a certain number of program graduates. The goal is to obtain job commitments equal to the number of people who are selected to participate in the program. The importance of obtaining placement commitments from the beginning cannot be overstated. If this placement campaign is not conducted very early in the program planning, the committee runs the risk of graduating persons who are left without jobs. The normal anxieties experienced by almost anyone faced with a major transition are likely to be greatly intensified by the uncertainties of completing the retraining without a job prospect.

In any event, the program plan should contain a contingency procedure that designates what happens to employees who have not been placed by the end of the training program. The options might include giving employees temporary assignments or additional training. As a last resort, graduates can return to their previous jobs until they are placed, but this is never a desirable alternative because trainees need to apply newly acquired skills as soon as possible or risk losing them. Furthermore, when graduates return to old jobs, their morale is likely to suffer.

A major consideration in establishing placement guidelines is how to handle salary and position levels. In some cases, placement opportunities may not match the candidates' previous levels. Jane Golden worked in a power supply test area in a company for many years testing components of products and doing some troubleshooting. Because of the advanced skills required to perform this work as well as her seniority in the position, Jane's wage rate was relatively high. The job was being phased down as the company moved toward automated testing, however, and Jane was accepted into a company-sponsored retraining program to prepare to be a computer programmer. Entry-level programmers made far less money than Jane was receiving before beginning the retraining. Under these circumstances, the company had to determine whether Jane would be forced to take a cut in pay and position or whether she would be allowed to maintain her previous rank and pay. Of course, the latter alternative is preferable to preserve morale. In Jane's case, the company decided to maintain her salary but told her that subsequent raises and promotions might be slower than in her previous job.

Candidate/Company Agreement

Some companies have determined that an agreement or contract between the candidate and the company is a useful tool to outline the expectations and obligations of both parties. When Hewlett-Packard launched its Planning for Partnerships pilot program in February 1986, company officials included a three-page agreement document that outlined the objectives of the program and the roles and responsibilities of the candidates and all other individuals involved. This agreement clearly spells out, for example, that students are expected to complete on-the-job training requirements and to keep both their current supervisors and the program team members informed of their progress. The company agrees to adjust work schedules and responsibilities, oversee the program, discuss training progress with the trainee, and assist in job placement (Casner-Lotto 1987).

Budget and Time Frame

The role of the retraining team in establishing a time frame and a budget for the program varies from company to company. Sometimes upper-level management turns over the budget and schedule restrictions to the retraining team. On the other hand, management may merely present the business rationale, program goals, and objectives to the team and ask the team to devise a plan that includes time and cost estimates. Under these circumstances, upper-level management usually retains the authority to make the final decision as to whether the budget is acceptable. Frequently, the committee is asked to submit several variously priced options from which managers can choose. In any case, the program team members almost always will be responsible for fleshing out the budget details and establishing a specific schedule as they develop the other components of the plan.

Developing the Curriculum Plan

Although all components of the retraining process are important, the curriculum is the heart of the program and must be developed with great care. Once team members make preliminary decisions concerning the curriculum so that they can establish selection criteria, their next task is to expand the details of the plan.

An effective curriculum plan must be based on an accurate profile of the prospective trainees and a clear set of training objectives that are determined by the required skills and levels of competency identified initially in the retraining plan. The curriculum plan should begin by reviewing the training objectives and describing each component of the curriculum. These descriptions should identify the course content, the teaching method, and the completion criteria for each course or module.

Curriculum Components

The first task in developing the curriculum plan is to identify the components to be included, considering the broad range of skills that are needed for successful job performance. The program also may require additional courses that address special circumstances facing the trainees. For example, if trainees have not been in school for a while, they probably would benefit from a class on study skills. Likewise, because most retraining programs are accompanied by increased pressure on trainees, a module on managing stress might be included in the program. If the trainees are making a particularly significant transition such as moving from factory work to office work, the team should strongly consider adding modules that address the psychosocial side of the passage from one career to another. The program might incorporate some methods for covering the issues of professionalism and career planning to supplement more technically oriented classes.

Generally these kinds of modules fall into three stages. As trainees enter the program, they participate in classes on study skills and dealing with change, which are part of the *entry skills*. A second set of program issues focuses on trainees' professional development and can be scattered throughout the program. Topics such as time management, communication skills, and professionalism fall under this *professional development* category. Finally, topics addressing the transition from the training to the new jobs should be scheduled near the end of the training program. The *transition to job* category includes activities such as career planning and individual counseling (Cheatum 1985). These three categories of supplemental modules cannot be overlooked in the curriculum plan. They are as crucial to trainees' transition as are the technical courses.

A secretarial retraining program that was conducted for a group of production employees in a large, manufacturing firm illustrates the use of supplemental modules. Ten women and fifteen men ranging from twenty-five to forty-five years of age participated in the program. They all had completed high school, but none had attended college. All had been out of school for at least seven years and some for much longer. Most of them had never worked in an office environment and were apprehensive about the transition. The men had some ambivalence about going into a profession that is predominantly female, and the women had some concerns about working with the men. They all worried about whether they would be accepted for a new position once they completed the training. The retraining team decided to provide some modules in the curriculum to address these issues. During the first week of the training one of the program's instructors taught a class on returning to the classroom. The students learned about how to listen to lectures, take notes, organize their homework, and handle their test anxiety. In addition, a counselor was hired to work with the trainees and spent an afternoon discussing with them the changes in their lives. They talked over their feelings about becoming secretaries, with a special emphasis on the sensitive male-female issues. The counselor returned the second week for a follow-up discussion with the group and, subsequently, was available one day each week for individual counseling sessions.

An entire week was set aside for professional development classes and activities about halfway through the program. During this week, the program manager, along with some of the company's

Developing the Curriculum Plan

secretaries, presented different aspects of the profession. For example, they described a normal day on the job in a variety of departments. They also talked about office etiquette and managers' expectations of secretaries. In addition to this professional orientation, the trainees took classes on communicating over the telephone, working with others, and managing time.

At the end of the retraining program, the counselor met with the group to discuss the move to the new job. They talked about how to reduce anxieties and adjust to new managers and co-workers. Each trainee had a meeting with the program manager to discuss their strengths and weaknesses as they left the program. They also talked about career goals and steps they could take to attain those goals.

Course Objectives and Content

The complete curriculum plan includes an outline of the objectives and course content for each component, with complex and lengthy courses broken down into topical units and specific objectives for each unit. The unit objectives outline the level of the information that the trainee needs to master. The mastery level can be determined by assessing what the student is expected to do with the knowledge or skill that the course addresses. Consider the various levels of competencies that are needed for technical writing. At the most basic level, writers merely may need to know how to proof documents by identifying incomplete sentences or spelling errors. At a higher level, writers may be required to correct the mistakes that they find. At a still higher level, they may need to be able to actually reorganize and rewrite documents. Each of these three types of tasks requires a different degree of mastery of the technical writing skills. If a course is to adequately prepare trainees for their prospective jobs, the course objectives and content should be matched to the tasks that trainees are expected to perform on the job.

Measurement Methods

In developing the components of the curriculum, planners must provide for measuring learning. The most popular approach in the traditional classroom is to administer tests, and for some of

Planning and Administering the Program

the courses in the retraining curriculum, testing also may be appropriate.

The use of this measurement method, however, requires some additional decisions. First, tests can be either informational or performance based. If trainees in a computer programming retraining class are to be tested, will they be asked to respond to questions about programming, or will they be asked to actually write a successful program? The proper form of testing depends on what trainees are expected to do on the job. If they will need to write programs, then they should be tested on their ability to perform this task rather than on their general knowledge of the process.

The team also should determine the form of grading that is to be used on the tests and how to provide feedback to trainees concerning their performance. If the course objectives call for students to achieve an established level of competency, then a pass-fail grading system is adequate. Even so, instructors should provide students with regular feedback on their progress throughout the duration of the course. The outcome of the final pass-fail decision should not come as a surprise to the student.

Although the pass-fail system works in many cases, a more refined grading system is sometimes preferable. If the trainees have several types of job options that vary in the levels of skills required, then a grading system would be useful for matching the students with the job. Returning to the example of training technical writers, suppose that the program includes classes on proofreading and separate courses on editing documents, and students receive a grade ranging from A to F for each class. At the end of the training, some of the graduates are to be placed in jobs that require them to rewrite documents and others are to work as proofreaders. Students who receive the highest grades in the editing classes would be the best candidates for the higher-level writing jobs. A pass-fail grading system does not produce a sensitive enough evaluation of the students to help with this kind of placement, and in this case, letter grades would be essential.

Of course, students should understand how their grades affect placement decisions. Trainees became extremely upset with the program manager when they were not told that their grades were being shared with prospective managers. They felt that an unspoken

Developing the Curriculum Plan

confidentiality agreement between the student and the instructors had been violated. These issues should be discussed with students at the beginning of the program.

Once they make the measurement decisions for the individual courses, planners are left with the task of outlining the criteria required for completing the program. In some cases, they may decide that the trainees must merely pass all of the courses in order to complete the program. In other cases, they may choose to set higher standards and require a level well above passing. For instance, if letter grades are used for the courses, they may require a grade of C or above in each course. Some programs include a set of competency tests that the trainees must pass at the end of the training in order to complete the program. In any event, the curriculum plan should include a measurement method for each course as well as a set of criteria for completing the program.

Teaching Methods

A primary task in curriculum development is to decide how courses are to be taught. Fortunately, educational research and modern technology provide the curriculum planners with a variety of delivery options to consider. At times, however, the flashy training systems may be appealing merely because they are novel or high tech. The best approach to choosing a delivery system is to examine training objectives and trainee characteristics and not be taken in by novelty.

If the trainees vary to a large degree in aptitude and experience, then a self-paced training approach is most effective, but the individualized system probably is inefficient if the group is fairly homogeneous in abilities. Of course, the nature and level of the skills that the training is to address also affects the choice of delivery system. On the rare occasion where the training objective is to familiarize students with concepts rather than to teach them to perform tasks, a traditional classroom style format probably is suitable. The objectives of most retraining programs, however, require trainees to perform tasks in addition to learning concepts. For achieving performance objectives, delivery systems such as interactive video training, roleplaying, supervised on-the-job experiences, or other hands-on approaches are more likely to work.

The objectives of most retraining courses focus on the acquisition of both concepts and skills, so planners usually need to choose a combination of delivery methods. However the subject matter is taught, trainees must have the opportunity to practice using what they are learning. In fact, research on adult learning has shown that older students acquire new information and skills more readily when they can see how these skills will be used on the job. Straight classroom delivery often falls short of successfully preparing the trainees for their new jobs, but some type of on-the-job training combined with the classroom training goes a long way toward enhancing the effectiveness of a retraining project.

Additional Curriculum Considerations

After planners have decided what topics to cover in the training program and how to teach those topics, their curriculum plan is almost complete. One major decision remains, however: They must determine who will teach the courses. Large companies that already have ongoing educational programs may be able to provide course development and instruction in-house. However, before choosing this avenue, the committee should check carefully to see if the content, materials, media, and time frame match the objectives of the retraining program. Furthermore, the committee must consider whether the company's standard courses meet the special needs of the trainees. Even if the course covers the subject matter that is needed for the retraining program, the level and pace of the course may not fit the abilities of the trainees. Sometimes, due to the unique nature of the retraining experience, the company needs courses that are specifically developed for the program in order to achieve its objectives. Then the issue is whether to develop the training internally or purchase the services of outside educational providers. This decision usually requires an assessment of the company's internal training capabilities as well as the availability of external resources.

Once the curriculum plan is in place, it should be reviewed to make sure that it does not overlook the special needs of participants who often undergo a major and rapid transition as a result of the retraining process. Not only are participants likely to be back in the classroom for the first time in years, but they often face the challenge of changing their professional identities. The assembler who retrains to become a computer programmer must learn programming languages and also must change his or her entire approach to work. Different attire, new behavior, and unfamiliar self-management styles are required for a successful transition to the new job. Moreover, the individual usually has left co-workers behind and sometimes must face relocating on completing the retraining. Planners must keep these issues in mind when designing the details of the program and consider how they can minimize the stress involved in the transition. In addition, they should review the curriculum from the framework of the following factors:

1. Compatibility with long-term skill needs;
2. Projected success and failure rates;
3. Reasonableness of the evaluation and completion criteria;
4. Reasonableness of time requirements.

Announcing and Publicizing the Program

The manner in which the retraining program is announced as well as the subsequent publicity that it receives establish the tone for the entire endeavor. Because beliefs about job security and change throughout the company can be affected by perceptions of the program, how employees learn of the project can influence its success or failure. Indeed, the communication strategy for the program can affect the morale and attitudes of everyone in the organization because an effective strategy can substantially lift company spirit even in the most challenging business climate.

One of the keys to a thorough communications plan is consistency in describing the program, and this coherence can be achieved only if the communications strategy is carefully constructed. The scheme should include details concerning timing and wording of messages, as well as who should receive the messages and how they should be delivered. Before preparing a plan, the drafters should be thoroughly familiar with the root causes and nature of the changes. For example, the retraining program may have been initiated because of the company's desire to maintain a competitive position in a dynamic industry, or the program may be the result of labor-management negotiations. With a full understanding of the rationale, drafters of the plan can design effective methods for communicating with managers, employees, and the public. The communications strategy should cover the following points:

1. How the program rationale will be communicated to management;
2. How managers should discuss the program with their employees;
3. How the program will be publicized internally to various audiences;
4. Whether information will be communicated outside of the company.

The most important audiences to address through the communications strategy are the managers and the employees. Although the information is essentially the same for both audiences, the approach to communicating the message may differ slightly for these two groups. The third audience to consider is the general public, and the approach for this type of external publicity varies considerably from the internal strategy.

Messages for Managers

Initially, the most crucial information needed by managers is the business rationale for the project. Managers must fully understand background facts if they are to communicate effectively with their staff. Prior to a formal announcement of the program, the retraining team should hold an informational meeting for all managers. There they can describe the conditions that led up to the program and how the retraining falls within the company's long-term strategy and direction. Because retraining usually is precipitated by changes within the economy, the industry, or the company, managers should be acquainted with this context. The team should be prepared to address any additional effects that these changes are likely to have on company policies and personnel. The meeting leaders should distribute an information packet that contains the following:

1. An advance copy of any internal or external announcements;
2. Explanations of what is going to happen and why;
3. Instructions on how to inform employees;

4. Hypothetical questions and answers that will enable managers to address employees' concerns.

Messages for Employees

The goal for communicating with employees is twofold: to develop understanding of the program and support for its objectives and to elicit applications for the program. The key task in designing messages for employees is to explain the change in an accurate and upbeat fashion. Media devices such as bulletin board displays, employee publications, meetings, and videotapes are helpful in supplying information about the program. One company with an outstanding record in creating a positive climate for retraining likes to prepare videotapes depicting success stories of employees who have adapted to past changes. They reinforce these scenarios regularly and frequently, conveying their continuing commitment to the growth and development of company employees.

When it began its retraining program, Hewlett-Packard encouraged communication between potential candidates and company officials in several ways. Officials instructed personnel managers in the departments faced with change to describe the program to employees. They also talked to the staff about shifts in the long-term climate, the effect on the company, and the need for retraining. The company held group meetings where people from expanding areas within the corporate structure described their jobs and answered questions, and interested employees were given tours of the divisions with job openings (Casner-Lotto 1987).

Messages for the General Public

The first question to address when thinking about approaching the community at large is whether the general public is interested in the retraining in the first place. If the retraining requires large numbers of people to leave the community for jobs at other company sites, community leaders are likely to be concerned. In fact, even if the company does not plan to make a formal announcement of its retraining plans, the local media are likely to ask for information. They are almost always interested in company decisions that could potentially affect employment levels, real estate values, or general economic activity in their regions. Therefore, if the community is likely to be affected in any way by the retraining program, a retraining team should work closely with the company's communications area to determine how and when to impart information. Even if the team decides not to approach the local press with information about the program, it should develop a contingency plan to use if the press comes to them.

In designing communication strategies for any audience, team members should keep in mind that events that they consider to be "positive" can temporarily cause disconcerting side effects. For example, while employees are being trained, managers may be temporarily short-handed and therefore may develop negative reactions to the program. Similarly, managers may resist filling vacant positions with trainees because they consider them to be less qualified than more traditional candidates. The families of trainees may pressure them to drop out of the program because of time demands that take them away from the family. Community leaders may respond negatively to programs that would lead to an exodus from the region or an influx into the area. The communications strategy should anticipate possible reactions and prevent negative repercussions.

Implementation

Implementing the retraining program can be accomplished with ease if the retraining team has done its work in developing the plans. Nevertheless, as the project unfolds, unexpected incidents occur from time to time. Although the entire retraining committee should be available for responding to crises, the program manager is the key player in providing advice and assistance throughout the execution of the plans. This individual serves many functions, including trainees' advocate and liaision between the trainees and other program administrators. In fact, students should feel that the program manager is willing to do anything within reason to help them succeed. For example, when Bill Mason suffered from an attack of acute appendicitis and was ill for three weeks, he was certain that he would have to drop out of the demanding retraining program. He had already completed three months of the program and felt that the time had been wasted; he was understandably upset. His program manager worked with the instructor to come up with a plan for allowing Bill to stay in the program. The instruc-

Implementation

tor's lectures were taped and delivered to Bill's home every evening. The company loaned him a personal computer so that he could complete his assignments at home. Because he was not able to keep up with the rest of the class completely from his home, Bill received help from a tutor when he returned to the classroom. Thanks to the efforts of the program manager in making these arrangements, as well as Bill's determination to catch up with his classmates, he was able to complete the course and continue with the program.

Monitoring the Instruction

If courses are delivered by people external to the company, the program manager, in cooperation with the education team member, must monitor the classroom activity. When companies completely turn over the instruction to an external provider, training can be either not relevant to the program objectives or out of place in the company culture. To avoid this predicament, the retraining team cannot lose track of what is happening in the classroom. Also, managers throughout the company should be informed periodically of the program's status and progress. Guidance for keeping managers updated should come from the team's communications plan.

Providing Feedback

Throughout the program, instructors and the program managers must provide feedback to the trainees at regular intervals. Although feedback is always significant in the process of training, it is especially important in retraining programs because trainees are likely to experience much anxiety related to the entire transition. If they are to perform well in the program, anxiety must be controlled through regular feedback and much individual reinforcement and encouragement.

Tracking Reactions

All members of the retraining team should be alert to signs of potential problems as the program proceeds. To assist in preventing crises, the communications area must monitor reactions throughout the company from the time that the program is announced until its completion. This continual tracking picks up early signals of trouble and negative reactions to programs that often can be attributed to misunderstandings and rumors. A carefully implemented communications strategy can prevent the proliferation of misinformation.

Evaluation

Evaluating the short-term and long-term outcomes of training programs is often neglected, frequently because of the time and expense involved in collecting data for thorough follow-up. On the other hand, the *lack* of a thorough appraisal can be even more costly if ineffective programs are repeated. In addition to wasted outlays for administering the program, there are other less obvious yet equally significant costs of ineffective training. Trainees may not be as productive on their new jobs or may make expensive mistakes. The commitment to use the results to evaluate the program and to act on the results to modify future projects can save the company money. A thorough evaluation consists of three types of assessments: achievement of immediate training goals, accomplishment of the business goals, and analysis of the long-term effect on careers.

Evaluating Training Effectiveness

The first step in evaluating training effectiveness is to assess whether the short-term program objectives have been met. This task is relatively easy to perform if measurement criteria were established in the retraining plan and data were collected throughout the program. The first part of the assessment should address whether the training objectives were accomplished according to the curriculum plan. Pertinent to these objectives would be whether the desired number of trainees demonstrated the required competencies for completing the program and whether the graduates could perform their new job responsibilities.

Coupling objective measures with subjective reactions to the program gives trainees the opportunity to evaluate the program immediately on graduating and again after a few months on the job. At the conclusion of the training, they should assess the instruction, classroom activities, selection and placement processes, course materials, and level of management support. After they are on the job for awhile, they should discuss the relevance of the training to the jobs they are performing. They also should be asked about the overall transition from classroom to job and how they feel about the entire retraining and career changing process.

Assessing Whether the Program Met Business Goals

The process of determining whether the program effectively fulfilled business goals is usually more complex than calculating whether training objectives were met, and the difficulty often depends on how clearly the business rationale was outlined in the first place. Sometimes the rationale will be so clear that the assessment is straightforward. If the program was to reduce the numbers of people working in a certain area of the company, counting the numbers of people from that area who either completed the training program or took jobs vacated by program participants could serve as evidence of success or failure. On the other hand, if the original rationale was to stay competitive with rival companies, the committee will have a much more difficult time weighing whether the program directly led to that outcome. Studying the following issues could provide valuable information for the future:

1. Will the training increase the number of people in areas where skill shortages exist?
2. Do the skills that employees acquire prepare them to meet the company's long-term needs?
3. How did the program affect morale, productivity, employee relations, equal opportunity, and salary throughout the company?
4. Did the placement of trainees differ from the initial expectations?

Long-Range Effectiveness

Although the short-term effectiveness of the retraining is probably the company's greatest immediate concern, knowing what happens to the graduates in the long run can be helpful in planning future programs. The personnel department should establish a method for tracking the long-range career progress of the trainees by monitoring their performance on the job, rate of promotion, and salary increases. In addition, their achievements and career progress should be compared to employees in equivalent positions who were hired from outside of the company. This information can increase the accuracy of the cost/benefit analyses that may be made as the company looks for solutions to future skill imbalances.

Special Issues

In order to increase the probability of conducting a successful program, the retraining committee should be aware of several potential pitfalls. A common mistake made by planners is to assume that planning steps are independent of each other. On the contrary, curriculum components, program budget, program time frame, and participant selection criteria are highly interdependent. All decisions about the curriculum, for example, depend on the time frame and budget, and likewise, the characteristics of participants entering training should influence the content and level of the courses.

If one objective of the program is to teach word processing, the number of courses and the length of time required to meet that objective depends on whether the participants already know how to type and the previous experience they have had with computers. Of course, the participant profile is determined by the selection criteria. If the time frame for training is short, then program planners should probably choose candidates who already have a strong foundation on which the training can build. Sometimes the budget and time frame are established from the outset by the upper-level managers who initiated the program, and under these circumstances, the retraining committee must operate within constraints. Program planners often try to pack too many classes into a limited interval. To further doom their efforts, they select participants who do not have suitable backgrounds and therefore cannot comprehend the material presented in the training program, and that guarantees failure from the outset. A second major error that program planners make is to begin training before completing planning. The success of retraining programs depends heavily on mapping out the details for all aspects of the retraining program. Therefore, the committee should expend a great deal of effort in developing the retraining program plan and should not jump into implementing the program before planning is completed.

Summary and Implications

Summary and Implications

The success of any retraining program is directly related to the care that goes into the planning of the program. The first step in careful planning is the selection of a team of staff members to oversee the entire program from beginning to end. If the program is to be large scale and long term, these staff members should represent a variety of areas within the company, including labor unions, personnel, education, communications, and departments to which trainees will be assigned on completion of the program. Key to the success is the selection of a program manager to coordinate and oversee all of the team's activities. It is critical that one person play this role through all stages of the program from the first day of planning to the final evaluation of the completed program. This person provides consistency for the program itself but, as important, is a significant link between the team and the trainees. A change in personnel can be very disruptive to both the program and the morale of trainees.

In every step of the program planning, team members should not lose sight of the overall goals of the company, the program, and the trainees. The program represents change to the trainees and will significantly affect their lives and their belief in the company. The committee should not limit the course goals to technical skills necessary for trainees to successfully compete in their new jobs. Self-management skills and functional skills such as problem solving also are important to develop a well-rounded employee who is technically proficient and can adjust to the new work environment.

A careful selection process is needed to determine which employees are most appropriate for the program. Whenever possible, the program should be voluntary to ensure motivation and enthusiasm, but even in voluntary programs the committee must determine the criteria by which interested employees will be selected. This requires careful review of aptitudes, skills, and backgrounds. Carefully selecting appropriate trainees and coupling trainees with appropriate courses for their skill levels and future needs will ensure the success of the trainees in their new jobs.

It is critical that trainees know that successful completion of the program guarantees them a new job within the company. The goal of the committee should be to obtain job placement for each of the people accepted into the program, and the committee should have these assurances before the program begins. At the very least, management should guarantee that a certain number of the program graduates will be offered positions. The guarantee of job placement is important to the success of the program and to the reduction of the normal anxieties associated with change.

The committee needs to be aware of the importance of announcing and publicizing the program. If a member of the communications staff is not part of the committee, members should work with that staff in developing a marketing strategy. The manner in which the program is announced can affect the morale and attitude of everyone in the organization. The committee also should anticipate and plan for local press interest in the program. Because the program represents change within the company and indicates a growth in or decline of jobs in specific departments, it affects the local economy and will spark community and therefore press interest.

Too often companies do not carry the program to its most logical and useful conclusion: a thorough evaluation of the training effectiveness. Both short-term and long-term effects of the program must be analyzed to correct any weakness or bolster the strength of future programs as well as ensure that the curriculum and selection process meets the needs of the company and the trainees.

References

Casner-Lotto, J. 1987. Hewlett-Packard's Partnerships for New Careers. In J. Rosow, Director, *Training for New Technology: Part IV, The Continuous Learning/Employment Security Connection*. Scarsdale, N.Y.: Work in America Policy Study Institute, p. 32.

Cheatum, V. *Personal Communication*, April 1985.

Hemmens, K. 1987. "Linking Training with Job and Income Security." In J. Rosow, Director, *Training for New Technology: Part IV, The Continuous Learning/Employment Security Connection*. Scarsdale, N.Y.: Work in America Policy Study Institute.

Morano, R., and J. Leonardi. 1987. "Xerox'x Critical Skills Training Program: A Commitment to Training Pays Off." In J. Rosow, Director, *Training for New Technology: Part IV, The Continuous Learning/Employment Security Connection*. Scarsdale, N.Y.: Work in America Policy Study Institute.

Pava, C. 1983. *Managing New Office Technology*. New York: Free Press.

CHAPTER SIX

Facilitating Transition: *Smooth Endings and New Beginnings*

RETRAINING programs are the result of widespread changes in the marketplace. Shifts in products, technologies, markets, or strategies can affect every level of the corporate structure. All employees, from top executives to line workers, experience various degrees of concern, curiosity, and confusion when faced with changes in their work lives. Just as policy makers reflect seriously on shifts in the marketplace, so should they carefully consider the effect of change on their own employees. Retraining programs are not isolated events and must be carefully woven into the entire process of transition that faces the company.

In this fast-paced marketplace, companies would do well to anticipate changes and plan for the reallocation of their workforce. As with all major projects, the most successful retraining programs grow slowly and are part of a carefully created environment that tempers anxiety and fosters enthusiasm for the challenges presented by change.

Keeping Up with Change: Career Planning

One of the most significant challenges for all companies is to convince employees of the need for career planning and lifelong learning. Presently, dramatic transformations in technologies and business strategies make complacency dangerous. None of us can be sure that our skills will always be in demand and that we can remain in the same job or profession for life. Over the course of a work life, each of us will undoubtedly be faced with the challenge of transition more than once. If these changes catch us by surprise, we will not be prepared to cope with the required adaptations. In fact, unexpected changes can exert enormous emotional costs on individuals as they become paralyzed by anxiety. Often, the results are depression and loss of productivity. In addition to emotional upheavals, unprepared workers frequently have to pay the price of losing their jobs because they do not have the right skills for adapting to the changing workplace. Major modifications can have devastating effects on a company as anxiety and insecurity escalate while morale and productivity drop.

Although the major responsibility for keeping up with shifting demands rests with individuals, businesses can contribute to their employees' preparation for change by establishing a climate that encourages continuous career growth and development. The employees must receive the message that the firm's competitive position depends on a workforce that can adjust to new conditions. The company leaders must communicate to employees that they are responsible for career planning and that the obligation for keeping abreast of change and updating their skills is part of the job.

In turn, the company should commit to fostering employees' growth and development. After all, the employees do not have complete control over their careers. Managers and boards of directors routinely make decisions that affect jobs. Furthermore, forces outside of the company such as shifts in consumer tastes, government regulations, and increased competition can affect the company's direction, which, in turn, can alter jobs. Although employees must devise plans that are adaptable to change, companies can help by making training and retraining central to the organization. For businesses willing to make serious commitments to human resource planning, the goal is to make these undertakings "business as usual." Moreover, the company can promote these activities by linking them to opportunities for growth and development.

The decision makers within a company can significantly assist employees by keeping them informed about prospective modifications within the industry and within the company. Although these messages should be as upbeat as possible, management should be honest about the potential negative implications of the changes rather than only highlight the benefits. After all, career plans are useful only when they are based on accurate information. Therefore, the degree of control that employees can exert over their work lives depends on their access to valid information about their professions, industry, and company. To understand the full picture, people need to hear not only the good news but also the bad news. Thus, if companies are committed to aiding their employees' career growth, they are obligated to keep them apprised of circumstances that might affect their jobs.

Self-Assessment

The foundation for the career plan is the personal data that comes from a thorough self-assessment. Although this self-appraisal is important for everyone in the company, the process is especially critical for those employees whose skills may soon be obsolete. The knowledge that comes from examining oneself becomes the foundation for building new careers. Priorities must be clear as individuals construct career goals and action strategies. Furthermore, employees need to examine their own strengths and weaknesses and to identify their skills so that their goals will be realistic. The company can help employees prepare for change by assisting with the process of examining these issues.

Both training experts and managers can effectively contribute to self-appraisal. Personnel and training departments often first spark the employees' realization of the need for assessment by offering career planning seminars or even individual counseling. They also may be able to provide direction to the employees by teaching a process for self-assessment. Managers also play a critical role as employees begin the process because they most readily know the strengths and weaknesses of their people and can assist as they begin the difficult task of sizing up their qualifications.

Self-evaluation for career purposes cannot be separated from an assessment of life priorities. Because time and energy are limited, each of us has to decide how work fits with other aspects of our lives. As employees examine their priorities, they decide what activities they value most. Individuals must decide how many hours they are willing to devote to work compared to their other commitments. Frequently, retraining programs and the careers that follow are much more demanding than are the jobs that trainees left. These increased responsibilities at work affect other areas of their lives. They may find that they will have less time and energy for

Facilitating Transition

family, friends, and leisure activities and are likely to experience more stress from increased work pressures. Therefore, people who are considering job changes must weigh both demands and benefits.

John Wilson worked in the assembly area of a plant that manufactures air conditioning engines. When the company executives decided to upgrade the technology, they also initiated a retraining program to teach workers to maintain the new machines. The new jobs, however, required the maintenance retraining graduates to work swing shifts and long overtime hours. Although this program certainly appealed to John, he felt a strong need to be home with his children in the evenings and decided not to apply to the maintenance program. Another assembly worker, Mary Bradley, applied to the program after she decided that the opportunities for career growth were important enough to her to sacrifice evenings to the job. These decisions were based on the individuals' own priorities.

Quite often, retrainees not only make sacrifices once the new jobs begin but also give up a great deal of time for the duration of the retraining. A large midwestern bank decided to offer a computer programming retraining project to its employees. The goal was to move people from jobs with an oversupply of workers such as teller positions into the rapidly expanding field of programming. The training program was intensive and often required trainees to spend up to thirteen hours a day on their studies. Many weekends, students sat at computer terminals or pored over their books rather than resting or enjoying activities with their friends and families. After completing the training, the programmers continued to put in long hours performing mentally demanding tasks. Several noted that they often found it difficult to turn off the work at the end of the day. Before committing to these kinds of demanding training programs and careers, individuals must decide the price they are willing to pay for advancement.

Once the individuals have clarified where work ranks in importance in their lives, they have only begun the self-assessment process. The next step is to ascertain what is most essential to them in a job. Although most of us have several job characteristics that we desire, in all likelihood we will not find the ideal job that fulfills all our requirements and must perform the difficult task of determining which qualities are most important to us and what we are willing to give up at least temporarily.

For example, consider the choices Mary Bradley made in entering the maintenance retraining program. She was looking for an assignment that allowed her to develop new skills and offered the potential for career growth and advancement. She preferred to move to a position in an office environment, but this point was less important to her than the opportunities for promotion. In deciding to enter the maintenance retraining program, she was willing to delay her desire to work in an office because she thought that the maintenance program held great promise for career growth. She was able to make that tradeoff because she was using a clearly ranked set of values as a framework for her decision.

After establishing clear priorities, employees can turn their attention to assessing and identifying all of their skills. Although most of us may think that we could quickly devise a short list of our abilities, in fact, a thorough assessment may uncover many skills that do not immediately come to mind.

The skills analysis should include a listing of several types of abilities. Usually the first skills to come to mind are technical and associated with specific positions. Frequently, these skills are included in a job description such as typing, programming, filing, and assembling. But individuals should not overlook more general work skills, such as leading, delegating, managing time, taking initiative, and dealing with the public. These skills also are important to the career change process. Sometimes, general skills are transferable to new positions even when technical skills are not. For example, at first glance, the skills that blue-collar manufacturer employees have acquired on the plant floor do not seem to transfer to the white-collar professions. However, even if the technical skill requirements do not overlap, some of the more general skills might be quite useful in an office environment. The factory worker who formerly checked products for defects on the shop floor shares the skill of examining or inspecting with the secretary who proofreads documents. This does not mean that the inspector could become a proofreader with no training. Certainly this task involves skills in addition to spotting defects; among other things, a secretary must be able to spell in order to proofread adequately. Nevertheless, the product inspector and the secretary must both be able to attend closely to detail and spot irregularities as prerequisites for performing their duties.

Richard Bolles (1976), an expert in career planning, has argued that most people possess hundreds of skills but that they must perform skills awareness exercises to identify all of them. He has said that skills are not merely acquired through formal schooling and job experiences but also are developed through other life activities. People who chair committees in church or in community clubs certainly acquire the ability to lead groups even if they have not been formally trained and have not been in leadership positions at work. He has suggested, therefore, that the skills identification process should involve more than merely listing the classes taken in school or other formal training received. One way to do a thorough skills analysis is to closely examine each of the jobs held and activities participated in over the years. These enterprises should be broken down into tasks performed, followed by a cataloging of the skills that went into carrying out the required duties.

For example, Sheila Brown is a secretary in a medium-size service firm. Her responsibilities are varied. A normal day for Sheila may consist of typing correspondence, making travel arrangements for several of the consultants, setting up meetings with their clients, preparing and typing reports, and updating the consultants' calendars. She may also file contracts that come in from clients and occasionally send out newsletters and other types of mailings. Her inventory of skills would include word-processing, proofreading, telephoning, coordinating, communicating with a variety of professionals, remembering details, organizing, classifying and retrieving, researching, developing rapport, representing others' wishes accurately, and so forth. When Sheila first attempted to merely jot down her skills, her list was short, yet when she thoroughly analyzed the tasks she performs each day at work, her list expanded.

Another method is to describe significant achievements and identify the abilities that account for those successes. A person who has recently received recognition for a hobby or who has excelled in a sports event or has gained a leadership position in a social organization might outline the abilities, talents, and efforts that led to these accomplishments.

Once they have completed all of the self-appraisal steps, the employees should use this knowledge of their *priorities* and *skills* to establish career goals. The case of Richard Bennett illustrates how self-appraisal dovetails with career planning. Richard worked for a large manufacturing company located in upstate New York. His job was with a support group for internal computer users ensuring that computer-generated reports going to managers were correct. After several years in this position he wanted to try something new. Because the company was undergoing some technological and procedural shifts that ultimately would affect employees, the training and education departments offered a number of career-planning seminars to the employees. Richard went through the self-appraisal process within the structure of the seminar. First, he looked at his priorities. He had a wife and three very young sons to support, and his interests revolved around his family and church. Although spending time with his wife and children was important to him, he felt that he could sacrifice a little more of that time for a job with higher pay and greater potential for advancement.

In assessing his skills and interests, he concluded that he would like to build on his experience with data processing. In addition, he had acquired some experience in analyzing how organizations function by serving on a planning committee at church. He found that he really enjoyed devising plans to improve the efficiency of the operations of his relatively large church. After he completed the career planning seminar, he took his self-assessment to his manager and asked for some guidance in setting career goals and action strategies that would allow him to build on his interest in organizational assessment and his experience with computers. The manager recommended that he pursue the training that would prepare him to be a systems analyst. Together, they mapped out a strategy to achieve this goal within four years. The manager pointed out to Richard that he would have to sacrifice much time to training and might have to transfer out of the New York plant in order to get jobs that lead up to systems analysts' positions. After discussing these tradeoffs with his family, he obtained their support, and with the assistance of his manager and his company's education department, he began implementing his action plan. As this case points out, the first and most significant step in career planning is self-assessment followed by the establishment of goals and action strategies.

Richard's case also points out that a manager can play a significant role in providing employees with information and helping them plan realistically. Sometimes employees may overestimate their own abilities or set goals that are based on inaccurate assumptions about the company. Another way in which managers can aid employees is by counseling them on retraining options. They can look for information about programs that would fit their employees' career goals. As employees become interested in particular programs, their managers can assist them in assessing their chances of being selected and completing the retraining. As prospective trainees and their managers look at the selection criteria and prerequisites for training, they could develop strategies for overcoming any weaknessess that might hinder employees' chances of being selected for the program. The manager might recommend that they take courses through a local educational institution or that they acquire some relevant work experiences that would strengthen their candidacy.

At times, individuals may not be able to make career choices that are consistent with their highest priorities. In these situations, managers can guide individuals through an analysis of their options even when all alternatives have negative aspects. For example, retraining programs offered by large corporations often require employees to relocate after completing the program. In these circumstances, employees have to choose between moving to new locations or forgoing the retraining. In the most severe conditions, if they forgo the retraining because of the relocation requirement, they run the risk of eventually losing their jobs as their skills become outdated. Deciding among unwanted alternatives is difficult, and managers can help employees productively make decisions under such adverse circumstances by urging them to establish priorities within the imposed constraints. For example, the employee who is offered a job with lower pay or a transfer to another location must face this choice realistically but may feel paralyzed by such undesirable alternatives. Their anxiety inhibits their ability to act. They may require some prodding by managers if they are to act on their choices.

In summary, career management in the face of change is a difficult process, and yet thorough self-assessment and goal setting become even more crucial in swiftly changing circumstances. Although individuals often cannot control the forces that account for change, their understanding of their own priorities, skills, strengths, and weaknesses can give them a framework within which to make choices. Career management is the shared responsibility of employee, manager, and company, but the primary responsibility falls on the employee. All individuals are obligated to determine their own priorities and goals as well as to assess their own abilities and interests. The manager can be the catalyst for stimulating discussions pertaining to career opportunities, company trends, or training options. Furthermore, managers can counsel and guide employees as they move through the career planning process. They can provide employees with information, identify opportunities, and help employees determine whether they qualify for other positions.

Career planning does not create job opportunities, nor does it guarantee promotion. It can, however, help employees grow both personally and professionally, enhancing their value to the company and their qualifications for meeting the needs of the changing workplace.

Preparing the Company for Change

Retraining programs are frequently prompted by significant changes within a company. As company leaders decide how to introduce the concept of retraining, they must not forget that the change itself will have a major effect and cause great concern among employees. Events within a company that require people to approach their jobs differently can lead to widespread employee stress with negative consequences for the entire organization. Company policy makers should carefully design the implementation of those changes, keeping in mind that anxiety is an inevitable by-product of even the most positive transitions. Stress can be reduced, however, by wisely managing change. Successful strategies for directing transitions require two steps: analyzing the probable effect of the changes on people throughout the company and developing plans for enhancing the positive results and cushioning, if not eliminating, the negative repercussions.

In some cases, these steps can be accomplished by one or more top-level managers or by a transition team. It is possible that the retraining team also can serve the function of the transition team. In very large organizations that are introducing major changes, however, a separate transition team may need to conduct the overall organizational appraisal. This team should work closely with the retraining team to coordinate overlapping activities and responsibilities. For example, both the transition and retraining teams should work together to develop a communications plan for informing people about the changes and about the retraining programs. This is merely one of many areas that must be addressed jointly by the two teams.

Analysis of Impact

The initial step for the transition team to take is to inventory how the changes will affect people throughout the company. The first part of the appraisal should look at the short-term and long-term benefits to the employees. Questions to be addressed include the following:

Are some jobs likely to become easier or more interesting?
Will the changes increase productivity? For whom?
Will the changes promote opportunities for career growth and development? For whom?

The second part of the appraisal looks at what people have to lose as a result of the changes. Questions to be addressed include the following:

Will some people lose their jobs?
Will more commitment or more energy be required? By whom?
Will anyone be moved to a new building or new location?
Will some people be working for new managers? With new colleagues?

The third part of the assessment should center around how people are likely to feel during the transition. Questions to address include the following:

Are some employees likely to feel a loss of control or a loss of their professional identity?
Will the status and power relationships shift within the company?
In what types of positions will people need to redefine their roles and relationships to others within the company?
Who is likely to resist? Why?

Preparing the Company for Change

The final part of the assessment should be a reading of the overall climate in which the changes are to be introduced. Questions to address include the following:

Do people have a history of trust and respect for each other and for the company?

Are people likely to believe what they are told about the changes?

Are employees likely to believe that the company is committed to helping them adapt to the changes?

In all likelihood, the degree to which changes are accepted or resisted will depend on the track record that the company already has established with employees. If the business has a history of inspiring loyalty, commitment, and trust in employees, the transition is likely to be smooth. Remember that a positive environment for change is not developed overnight.

Development of the Action Plan

Naturally, action plans for addressing the transition are based on the results of the impact analysis. The transition team should look for possibilities for enhancing the effects for each positive change. If the analysis indicates that some workers will become more productive as a result of the changes, perhaps the team should recommend salary increases or bonuses. If some employees will receive training in order to perform new roles created by the changes, the team could examine the possibility of arranging for these employees to receive certification or educational degrees as they achieve the training goals.

Next, the team should search for ways of preventing or minimizing the adverse effects of each item on the negative impact list. If some people are likely to lose their jobs, perhaps the team could arrange for outplacement assistance. If certain roles or relationships are to change dramatically, the team could set up informational meetings to help people redefine their function and status. A series of team-building activities could be implemented to help strengthen new working relationships. These examples represent only a few of the strategies that the team might design to facilitate employees' smooth transition during a period of change.

Of course, successful implementation of changes requires a

thoughtful and sound communications plan. The transition team, along with the retraining team, must concentrate on constructing methods for informing people about the changes in a way that will, at a minimum, reduce anxiety, and, optimally, create enthusiasm for the new circumstances. Company leaders frequently find that one of the most effective ways to prevent problems is to educate managers on how people normally react to change and to teach the managers how they can assist their employees. Many firms offer help sessions to employees who are most likely to be affected by the changes.

Facilitating the Retrainees' Transitions

Although many people throughout a company are likely to be affected by the changes that lead to retraining, the individuals most directly affected are the retrainees themselves. Because the transition that these people face is likely to be dramatic, they should receive special attention as the teams plan to facilitate change. When graduates of training programs describe their experiences, they point out that they face two separate transitions: short-term changes in their lives brought about by participating in the training program itself and more complex, long-term pressures caused by changing careers.

Alleviating the Stress of Training

As employees first begin the retraining process, their immediate concerns center on the training program. The program often is the first time in many years in which they have returned to the classroom as students. They frequently worry about comprehending lecture material, taking adequate notes, competing with others, taking tests, and meeting assignment deadlines. Many programs are very demanding in that the training is compressed into a relatively short time frame. It is not unusual for trainees to spend thirteen to fourteen hours a day listening to lectures and completing assignments. More often than not, trainees are aware of the demands of the program from the outset but will feel frustrated and guilty about sacrificing time with friends and family in order to complete the program. For example, one new mother expressed remorse because she could not spend more time with her infant. Sometimes these sacrifices and pressures make the trainees feel overwhelmed and not in control of their lives.

It is clear that training and transition pressures can create high levels of anxiety in students. The anxiety is exacerbated in the classroom because when individuals are distressed, they often are unable to concentrate. Furthermore, they frequently lose sleep, which results in their not being alert during the day. These conditions could easily lead to failure even for students who are quite capable of learning under less tense circumstances. A former assembly worker who was studying to become a computer programmer expressed the feelings of most trainees about the pressures they face: "I feel so inadequate. My entire future depends on my performance in this class, and yet I can't seem to get my thoughts into gear. No matter how hard I work, I keep falling behind."

Because the negative consequences of too much tension can be severe, the retraining team should take steps to help trainees handle pressure. For instance, they can work out a formal plan for assisting trainees with personal problems that arise throughout the transitional process. One aspect of the plan should include training modules to help students develop skills for attacking the sources of their anxieties. A useful module could focus on developing skills for returning to the classroom. The instructor could include tips on studying, listening, notetaking, and overcoming test anxiety. Teaching students to manage stress and cope with change could be the goal of another set of modules.

Although this type of instruction can be useful, training modules alone often fall short of thoroughly addressing the trainees' needs. Therefore, some companies arrange for a counselor to be available to help with personal issues on an individual basis. At times, the retraining program manager may be capable of filling this counseling role. For the most part, however, someone with professional counseling expertise should be available. If a counselor is to be connected with the program, this person should be introduced from the beginning in a way that is not threatening to the trainees. The counselor could conduct training modules early in the program on managing stress and coping with change, which allows the counselor to develop rapport with the students. Subsequently, the counselor could offer additional modules at regularly spaced intervals throughout the program. At least periodic contact with all of the trainees is necessary for establishing trust; trainees are much more likely to share their personal problems with a counselor with whom they have spent time.

In addition to working directly with students, the counselor can also serve another important function. He or she can advise the program manager, instructors, and other retraining team members on the psychological issues involved in retraining and career transition. Through this advice, the people working with trainees on a day-to-day basis can become more sensitive to matters that are likely to affect their adjustment.

As discussed previously, the most crucial step that a company can take to relieve stress is to keep employees, and especially trainees, informed. During the program announcement and selection phase, managers should be prepared to share information with their employees pertaining to the length of the program, the selection criteria, the placement process, and career paths for graduates. In addition, the retraining program committee should hold at least one meeting for interested employees to respond to questions, after which managers should be responsible for obtaining answers to additional questions that arise.

Addressing the Complexities of Long-Term Stress

Although alleviating the immediate stress that students face during the training period is critical, often these short-term anxieties mask much larger fears that do not end with the training. The most common source of apprehension is uncertainty about the future as trainees face the challenge of moving into a new job. Despite their training, they are often crippled by an acute fear of failure. In many cases, a career change represents moving from an area where individuals feel very confident of their abilities to a new area where they feel inadequate.

The fear of failing threatened Larry Martin, who worked in the distribution department of a large manufacturing operation. His job was to monitor an automated stockroom containing small parts. He had worked for the company for fifteen years in a variety of positions associated with manufacturing but felt that his jobs had not been particularly challenging and that opportunities for growth were extremely limited. When he entered the company's secretarial

Facilitating the Retrainees' Transitions

retraining program, he knew that the company offered many opportunities for secretaries with word processing and computer skills. During the training program, however, he demonstrated high levels of anxiety, which sometimes made it difficult to study and take tests. He even started to develop physical symptoms as a result of this stress. The program manager noticed that the quality of Larry's performance in the classroom varied from day to day according to his state of mind. In discussing his anxiety with the counselor, Larry revealed that his buddies in the stockroom had really teased him about becoming a secretary and, in fact, had given him a pair of panty hose as a parting gift. For the most part, he had come to terms with entering a profession that is predominantly female, but he dreaded "flunking out" of the retraining program and possibly returning to the stockroom to face the ridicule of his former co-workers. This fear of embarrassment was exacerbated by uneasiness about being a novice again. He was forty years old and used to being an experienced employee, particularly "teaching the new guys the ropes" in the stockroom. As a result of his lack of knowledge and skill at the beginning of the program, he felt inept and became convinced that he would fail in his endeavor to become a secretary. In reality, he had showed more promise at the beginning of the program than many of his classmates.

It is natural for people who enter a program to lack many skills that they ultimately will need to perform their jobs. However, like Larry, many trainees who have worked in the same position for a number of years are uncomfortable with the feelings of incompetence, which frequently results in an exaggerated fear of failure. The counselor was able to help Larry come to terms with his overwhelming anxiety about his own capabilities. Fear of failure is not unusual and many students experience similar anxieties, particularly older students who have been in the same job for many years. As one person said, "After thirty-five years in one type of job, I have to start all over. Is this possible? I think so, but I'm scared."

Trainees are also worried about the demands that will be placed on them as they move from highly structured, routine jobs into demanding, unstructured professions. These new careers are likely to demand more independence as well as new attitudes toward appropriate on-the-job behavior. Trainees worry about what they

Facilitating Transition

will have to do to become "professional." They are usually acutely aware that the acquisition of new technical skills alone will not ensure their successful transition. They are uncertain about their new image and how it meshes with their own personalities.

A critical source of long-term stress can come from misunderstandings and pressures within the trainees' personal relationships outside work. For example, even when trainees have carefully determined what they are willing to sacrifice for the training, unforeseen events often occur in their private lives. Divorce, deaths, and other emergencies cannot always be avoided for the duration of the training. One trainee in a particularly demanding program experienced great anxiety because he could not be with his gravely ill sister.

As the students face uncertainty about the professionalism required in their new jobs, they also are unsure of how these changes will be viewed by family and friends. Because many programs prepare trainees to be professionals, participants often change the way they dress and talk and, in some cases, even the way they spend their leisure time. Take the case of Fred Smith, who worked for fifteen years on an assembly line. In his old job, Fred worked a regular forty-hour week and was paid double for overtime. He reported to work in blue jeans and performed repetitive tasks in a highly structured environment. On beginning to retrain to become a computer programmer, his entire work life changed. He was expected to wear a coat and a tie and to learn office etiquette. Part of his training included communications courses that emphasized the importance of proper grammar. He was told that he was expected to work until the job was completed and should not expect overtime pay for the extra hours. For a large part of the day, he was on his own to structure his work and study time. The program manager explained to all of the trainees that they should be "professional at all times." Although Fred welcomed the changes, his family teased him about becoming "uppity" as he attempted to adjust to these new demands.

The trainees' development of new professional identities can be stressful not only for them but also for the other people in their lives. Their family and friends may fear that they too will have to change or be left behind. Mark Bradford's story is another illustration of these hardships:

> I come from a small farming community and I find that some of my friends, relatives, and people I grew up with no longer feel comfortable around me since I started working in an office. Most of the time it doesn't bother me but with a few of my closest friends, it does. I lived next door to two of them until I was eighteen. Before I came to work here, my greatest ambition was to buy a bar and just have a good time. Now I find that I am more and more career motivated. I want to excel in this new job.

The dilemma for people like Fred and Mark is that they need the love and support of those who are close to them in order to ease the stress of their transition, yet their families and friends may withdraw from them because of their own insecurities and fears. Because insecurities tend to thrive when people feel uninformed and left out, the best approach for trainees is to keep those who are close to them involved in their transition.

This involvement on the part of all members of the trainees' families becomes particularly critical as the training program comes to a close. Often internal family stresses are at their peak then because the program has demanded long hours, forcing the student to spend less time with family and friends. On graduation, stress often remains as the student continues to experience change in his or her life. At this stage, it is important that the entire family understand the implications of the new job. The long hours demanded during the training program may be just as necessary during the early stages of the new job. Moreover, some programs call for graduates to relocate to another site—a contingency that their families may resist. Indeed, the relocation issue has led to the breakup of some marriages. Although these differences are difficult to resolve, trainees may be able to prevent some of the complications by discussing all of the details with their families prior to their enrollment in the program. The most distressful predicaments are created by people who do not include their families in their decisions to retrain.

Frequently, the failure to discuss the program details comes from the fear of conflict over some of the circumstances surrounding the retraining. In avoiding an immediate encounter, however, trainees increase the chances of greater discord when, at a later date, they are forced to let their families in on their plans. As a case in point, Jerry Mitchell experienced a great shock when, at the conclusion of the retraining program, his wife demanded a divorce because she did not want to relocate. He was extremely upset by what he claimed was an unexpected blow, even though he admitted that he had not discussed the relocation contingency with his wife until two weeks before the move was to take place but had known about it for months. She felt that he had deceived her and therefore reacted more strongly to the impending move than if Jerry had discussed it with her from the start. Of course, conferring with families from the outset does not always ensure against conflict, but it certainly invites problems when students fail to bring spouses and other family members into the deliberation of issues that directly affect their future.

Ultimately, although the company and retraining team can offer some assistance, the students learn to deal with their individual pressures in their own fashion. They realize that coping with many changes and adapting to new roles is difficult for almost everybody, and that they need to face what is happening to them realistically. Indeed, everyone involved with the program should understand the natural reactions to change. They should be aware that there is a difference between resistance to change and the normal expression of anxiety mixed with some grief during times of transition. William Bridges (1980) in his book *Transition: Making Sense of Life's Changes* points out that all transitions start with endings. People faced with change have to let go of the way things were and the way they viewed themselves in the past. This "unhooking" must occur if trainees are to realistically face the future.

In their confrontation with reality, the trainees need to assess what they can and cannot control. One of the reasons change is so stressful is that people lose a sense of command over their lives and their feelings of helplessness lead to anger or depression or both. Through assistance, they can learn to identify areas in which they are in control. At the same time, however, they must give up the frequently held, yet irrational, belief that, if they try hard enough, they can regulate everything. The key to effective coping rests with the trainees' abilities to achieve a sense of influence over some events and yet to learn to live with some inevitable and uncontrollable ambiguity.

Unfortunately, the training staff, in its attempts to encourage positive attitudes about the changes, sometimes unwittingly will

Facilitating the Retrainees' Transitions

promote the belief that everything about the career change will be ideal. The students will come to believe that, if they can just complete the retraining, all of their problems and stresses in every area of their lives will go away. Furthermore, in their attempt to embrace the changes students also may look at their old job versus their prospective new jobs in simplistic terms. They may come to believe that their previous jobs were completely unfulfilling and develop the expectation that the new job will be totally satisfying. These beliefs alleviate anxiety in the short run, but in the long run, trainees sometimes become depressed just at the time when they need to be especially energized so that they can adapt to their new jobs. This letdown can be particularly discouraging because it is unexpected.

Although some trainees are unrealistically positive about the changes, others are pessimistic if not resistant about everything. These reactions commonly occur in situations where programs have not been adequately "sold" to employees or in which their participation is involuntary. Neither the idealistic positive reactions nor the counterproductive negative responses allow trainees the best chance of successfully handling the transition. Trainees need to assess how the change is affecting their lives. They should ask themselves questions like the following:

What are the positive aspects of the changes?
What are the negative aspects of the changes?
What am I gaining as a result of the transition?
What am I leaving behind?
What are my hopes and fears for the future?
What aspects of the changes cause me stress?

As previously stated, the company can certainly provide support and guidance to the student during the job change. Perhaps the retraining team can recommend that the counselor provide some group sessions with students and family members. One company realized that the training program significantly reduces the amount of time students are able to spend with spouses and children. It compensated by inviting families to a special orientation session and then holding group social events periodically throughout the months of the program (Rosow and Zager 1987).

When graduates are faced with relocation, some companies have developed a variety of programs to assist the whole family with the move. One company made a videotape that featured families throughout the corporation who had relocated to various sites across the country. The families talked quite candidly about their experiences and offered practical advice on the move itself as well as a more personal discussion of the emotional upheavals that they faced as they left their familiar surroundings. Through the videotape, they provided a different perspective and fresh insight into how the move affected trainees' and their families. The company used the tape to spark discussions at a number of informal, informational meetings held for trainees and their families.

Other strategies for assisting families include

1. Assigning to each trainee and family a "host" family in the city where they will be moving. The host family corresponds with the trainee's family during their preparation for the move and assists them with learning their way around town once they arrive.
2. Providing job search assistance to the trainees' spouse. Frequently, the trainee will be part of a two-career family, and the move is disruptive to the husband or wife's career. Spouses are much more likely to adjust to relocation if jobs are available for them.
3. Sponsoring visits for the entire family to the new location so that the family can become familiar with its new city before they actually move.
4. Developing a directory of services within the new community. Newcomers like a listing of doctors, dentists, attorneys, mechanics, and others offering practical and necessary services.

The trainees' new managers also can ease stress through their acceptance of the trainees. Ideally, these managers are involved with the program from the beginning, have participated in the selection of the trainees, and made commitments to hiring them at that early point. However, sometimes such ideal conditions do not exist. At times, these managers not only have been uninvolved in the program but also resist hiring graduates because they would rather hire new people to fill vacant positions. If the company exerts pressure on them to take retrainees, they are likely to feel resentful. Their resistance can come from lack of information or doubts about the soundness of the program. They may believe that only the more traditional methods for training will work, such as obtaining a degree from a college or professional school. Moreover, people within their departments who did acquire more traditional training may express resentment and even may be reluctant to work with the retrained graduates. One key to avoiding these kinds of problems is ensuring that the program is sound and the goals are achievable from the beginning. Very early in the planning stage, the retraining team should develop an approach for generating understanding and support for the program.

At a minimum, the retraining team should ensure that managers form realistic expectations about program graduates. Managers need to be aware that their new employees probably will need special assistance at first and may need additional training. They should be informed of the specific apprehensions that trainees are likely to experience as they take on their new responsibilities and should be given tips on how to address these apprehensions. In the most successful programs, new managers cooperate fully with the retraining team and work closely with trainees who will be assigned to them. In one program, each trainee was assigned a mentor from the department where he or she would work on completion of the program. The mentor not only noted the trainee's progress but also kept the individual informed about projects and opportunities in the department (Rosow and Zager 1987).

A good way to ease the transition from the classroom to the job is to build an apprenticeship component into the program. Under these circumstances, retrainees learn how to apply what they have learned on the job while still officially in the training mode. They are likely to be less anxious, and the expectations of those for whom they are working are likely to be more realistic. When the transition from classroom to job is not abrupt, the graduates' fear can subside, leaving the company with an enthusiastic and thoroughly trained employee.

Summary and Implications

Retraining programs are prompted by shifts in business conditions and therefore must be addressed by many levels in the company. The most successful retraining programs grow slowly and are the

Facilitating Transition

result of careful planning and a corporate environment that prepares employees for change, particularly for long-term career planning.

Any career plan must begin with a personal exploration of individual skills, strengths, weaknesses, and priorities. Each employee should prepare such a listing. The company can encourage this self-assessment through career planning seminars or individual counseling. In any self-assessment plan, it is important to identify priorities that go beyond the job, such as needs of families or non–work-related goals. Skills too are not limited to those reflected in a job description but should include skills learned through hobbies, civic activities, or other experiences.

Employees can use the information gained from self-appraisal exercises to develop career goals. At this stage the company can be particularly helpful by providing employees with information about change within the company and the retraining program and with a realistic assessment of how the employee can best become part of the new opportunities. Career planning does not create job opportunities or guarantee promotion, but it can help employees to see more clearly how they can enhance their value to their company and achieve their own goals.

Change causes a certain amount of concern among employees, ranging from simple curiosity to outright anxiety. Company leaders should anticipate such concern and carefully plan the implementation of those changes. In cases of major change, a transition team may be needed in addition to the retraining team, although both groups should work closely and coordinate activities. The transition team should have the responsibility for assessing how the changes will affect people throughout the company and then develop a plan to maximize the positive results of the change, while preventing or minimizing the adverse effects. Again, it is critical that the company keep employees accurately informed of the effects of the changes. A carefully constructed communications plan can reduce anxiety and foster enthusiasm.

Of course, those individuals who experience the most anxiety during the period of transition are the trainees. During training, they face the stress of adjusting to their new status as students, long hours of studying, pressures from home, fear of failure, and concerns about the future. Some of these fears are often escalated, rather than alleviated, as students leave the training phase and move to new jobs. Although most employees develop individual coping skills, companies can help by providing professional counseling courses in study skills, the encouragement of managers, and support services such as help with moving and job placement for spouses.

References

Bolles, R. N. 1976. *What Color Is Your Parachute?* Berkeley, Calif.: Ten Speed Press.

Bridges, W. 1980. *Transition: Making Sense of Life's Changes.* Reading, Mass.: Addison-Wesley.

Rosow, J. M., and R. Zager. 1987. *Training for New Technology: Part IV, The Continuous Learning/Employment Security Connection.* Scarsdale, N.Y.: Work in America Policy Study Institute.

CHAPTER SEVEN

◆

Retraining the Older Worker: *Different Requirements?*

THE AMERICAN workforce is getting older. For the first time in history, teenagers in the United States are outnumbered by people age sixty-five and older. At the same time that the number of older Americans is swelling, the younger segment of the population is shrinking, indicating a likely shortage of new entrants into the workforce. In fact, 75 percent of the people who will comprise the workforce in the year 2000 are already working today. Demographers project that by 1990, between 12 and 20 percent of American workers will be at least fifty-five years old (Kaminski 1983). Indeed, the average age of the American worker has risen over the past decade, a trend that is expected to continue. Companies will become increasingly dependent on workers who are middle-aged or older.

Because companies will not be able to depend on hiring new people with appropriate skills as the workplace changes, they will need to retrain many of their existing employees, a large percentage of whom are likely to be at least middle-aged at the point when their skills become obsolete. As personnel plans are made and retraining programs are designed, decision makers should pay special attention to issues pertaining to older employees' training needs and their abilities to make transitions.

Why Retrain Older Workers?

The experience, maturity, and loyalty of workers who are middle-aged to older make them valuable assets to companies that develop

Why Retrain Older Workers?

practices that allow for their continued productivity, and yet many practices and policies are biased against older workers. Decision makers have tended to believe that retraining older workers is not cost effective because they do not remain in the workforce long enough to give the company a good return on its investment. This argument is losing its validity as economic and social circumstances encourage employees to remain in the workforce longer. As part of the personnel planning process, companies should assess the likelihood that workers will remain employed into their older years.

In addition to corporate America's increasing dependence on older workers, other indicators suggest that workers will choose to stay in the workforce longer. A major reason for making this prediction is weakness within the Social Security system. In 1962 the option for retiring at age sixty-two and receiving 80 percent of Social Security benefits was offered to American workers. Over the years, a large percentage of the labor force has chosen to take advantage of this offer. Economists fear, however, that as the ranks of the elderly increase and the numbers of young entrants into the workforce decline, not enough people will be paying into the Social Security system to support those who want to draw from it. The greater the number who choose early retirement, the heavier the financial strain on Social Security and Medicaid. Some argue that the fifty-five to sixty-four age group should be encouraged to continue to participate in the labor force to continue to contribute to the tax base rather than draw benefits from it. Various proposals aimed at salvaging the Social Security system have included suggestions that the benefits for early retirees should be reduced. Any substantial rate reductions are likely to have the effect of keeping people in the labor force longer. In fact, as long ago as 1981 a Harris poll corroborated the prediction that individuals plan to retire later compared with previous years (Harris et al. 1981).

In addition to arguing that the continuing labor force participation of older Americans will help ease the strain of Social Security, some claim that the contribution of their expertise is important to the nation's economic efficiency and to the gross national product. Indeed experts have predicted that older workers will increase the gross national product by $45 billion annually by 1990 and nearly $200 billion by 2005 (Kaminski 1983). Certainly, as the pool of younger workers and workforce entrants shrink, companies will rely more heavily on the continued participation and productivity of their older workers.

On the more personal side, older people today are healthier and thus in better shape to continue working than they were earlier in this century. If, as some have argued, perceptions of age should be increased by ten years, decisions made about people in their mid-fifties should be based on practices that used to apply to people in their forties. Moreover, now that traditional family ties are looser and older people are less likely to live near their children and grandchildren, they may extend their work lives in order to maintain social contacts (Rosow and Zager 1980). In sum, over the next decade, people are likely to choose to continue working longer for both monetary and psychological reasons.

Many workers who have left their jobs involuntarily subsequently have suffered both financially and psychologically. For instance, Barry Weis found that he was faced with early retirement at age fifty-eight. The large service organization that had employed him as a middle manager for thirty-five years was cutting back on personnel and his forced early retirement was part of this strategy. As the company restructured and eliminated entire layers in the bureaucracy, Barry was a casualty of reorganization. He was not prepared to deal with the loss of his job and felt that he had been cast aside by the company to which he had been loyal for nearly his entire working life. He wanted to continue working but found that other companies in the area were reluctant to hire someone at his age. Those companies that did consider his application were offering entry-level salaries far below his previous salary. The companies were not willing to pay for the seniority and experience that Barry brought from his former employer. He became frustrated and depressed.

Cases like Barry Weis's illustrate the extreme psychological costs of involuntary retirements, but the price that the company pays also can be high. Not only is the company losing the experience and expertise that the long-term employee possesses, but early retirement also carries with it the concrete expenses of pension payments. If the current trend toward early retirement continues, the costs of companies' pension systems will grow dramatically as larger numbers of workers reach the age where the early retirement option is available to them.

Thus, there are several reasons for human resource planners to consider the needs of middle-age to older workers as they develop their personnel and retraining strategies. First, the costs associated with early retirement may become prohibitive, and companies may cut back on this option, leaving a larger pool of older people in their employment. Second, age discrimination laws make it imperative for companies to develop policies and practices that are fair to employees of every age. Older workers have the legal right to retrain. Third, the experience, maturity, and loyalty of workers who are middle-age to older make them valuable assets to companies that give them a chance to continue to grow. Fourth, in the near future companies will need their middle-age to older employees because there will be a shortage of younger workers. It will be crucial that these employees possess the skills to meet the increasing demands of the modern workplace.

As part of the personnel planning process, firms should assess the numbers of middle-age to older workers who will be part of their workforce in the future and evaluate personnel policies as well as national trends that might affect the workforce participation of older individuals. Subsequently, they should determine the degree to which the middle-age to older workers will need new skills. Their analyses are likely to reveal that a large proportion of these employees will need to be retrained. Given these circumstances, program planners should pay special attention to the conditions that are conducive to older employees learning and making successful transitions.

Who Are Older Workers?

In order to address how to retrain older workers, company leaders have to determine who falls into this category. This task may not be as easy as it first appears. The categorization of "older worker" within the public sector seems to vary considerably. For example, the Administration on Aging considers anyone who is at least fifty-five years of age to be "older." On the other hand, the Department of Labor refers to anyone forty-five and above as a "mature worker," and the Age Discrimination in Employment Act sets a lower limit of forty years old.

In truth, the biological and psychological aging process varies from individual to individual. Factors such as genetics, life experiences, health, and attitudes determine how age relates to work performance. For the purpose of planning retraining programs, anyone who is age forty or above should probably be considered "older." There are several reasons for establishing this relatively young age as the lower boundary for the "older worker" category. Workers who have reached the age of forty frequently have been away from an intensive training environment such as the classroom for a number of years and are likely to differ from their younger counterparts in their approach to learning. If the training is formal, such as classroom training, participants who are in their forties or older are likely to approach the retraining with more apprehension and different learning styles than their younger colleagues.

For instance, Leonard Martin entered a retraining program for maintenance jobs in an automated assembly area. Leonard's performance in high school had been average, and he had scored very well on an aptitude test that was used as a screening instrument for the program. Nevertheless, Leonard was forty-two years old and had not participated in formal classroom education since high school. He had updated his skills over the years through on-the-job training and through short, concentrated training classes. The maintenance retraining consisted of a set of courses that were conducted by the local community college, which designed a curriculum to provide a strong theoretical base on which to build technical maintenance skills. Leonard had great difficulty with the theoretical classes. He found that he could not concentrate on material that did not seem to have an immediate relevance to the job. He did not really know how to take lecture notes and found that his attention often wandered off of the topic being discussed by the instructor. As a result, his anxiety as test days approached became debilitating. Although his younger classmates had some trouble with the theoretical classes, they were much more accustomed to dealing with lectures and test-taking. Leonard's eventual failure and removal from the program may have had more to do with his lack of recent classroom experience than with his actual ability to learn.

In addition to having been away from the classroom, people who are at least forty also differ from their younger colleagues in attitudes and values, and these differences affect their motivation to retrain and their disposition toward transitions. Many psychologists consider the early to mid-forties to be the beginning of midlife changes that are often fraught with shifts in priorities. It is at this point that many people comprehend that they may never realize the grand career and money-making dreams of their youth. As they attempt to come to terms with their own mortality, they become more introspective. They are likely to become less motivated by external forces such as what others think of them and more concerned with internal rewards and satisfaction. As a result of some of these changes, they are less likely to define themselves totally in terms of what they do for a living. In fact, studies have shown that overall satisfaction with life for those in later years is not as dependent on satisfaction with work as it is for younger people (Cohn 1979).

Bill Swartz's case illustrates this switch. Bill had worked in quality control for a large manufacturing company for twenty years. He was forty-eight years old and recently recovered from a heart attack when the company decided to change to statistical quality control. In order to keep his job, he had to enter a very stringent retraining program. Bill always had been ambitious and willing to work long overtime hours, but since his heart attack, his attitude toward work had changed. Although he was willing to enter the program, he was reluctant to give up his evenings to study. He worked hard during the day, and his performance in the program was adequate. His commitment to do his best was indicative of his positive attitude toward the program. Nevertheless, he set limits for how much time he would work at his studies. He was no longer willing to dedicate all of his energy to the job or to the training. Many trainees who are in their forties or older are likely to approach retraining with similar attitudes. Although most are willing to meet the demands of the retraining program, no matter how great, they are likely to experience high levels of stress if they are forced to give up a large percentage of their free time.

For these reasons, program planners should give special attention to the learning styles and approaches to transitions of employees forty and older who need to be retrained. If retraining programs are to adequately address skill imbalances, many should be predominantly filled with people in this older age range. After all, because older workers have usually been on the job for a while, they are more likely to have outdated skills. It is not that older trainees need constant attention and extraordinary consideration but that their unique and frequently invaluable characteristics call for consideration as retraining is planned.

Characteristics of Older Workers

Older workers have many qualities that are advantageous to their companies. They have lower rates of absenteeism and are at least as proficient interpersonally as are their younger colleagues. Furthermore, they tend to be more dependable and have higher levels of commitment to the job. Their maturity and experience allow them to bring stability to the workplace and enable them to serve as mentors and role models to younger workers. Nevertheless, decision makers tend to view older employees as less worthy of the training investment even though the fifty-year-old who is retrained could continue to work for twenty more years. Paul Barton, in his book *Worklife Transition*, argues that older workers are less attractive to employers because of a self-fulfilling prophecy. Companies usually train and retrain younger workers, so that older workers frequently are not prepared to deal with changes in the organization that require new skills (Barton 1982). As a result of their lack of skills, older workers may fear and resist change.

Take the case of Martha Struckman. She had worked in a clerical position for a medium-size service organization for many years. She was fifty years old when sophisticated office automation was introduced within her department. Unlike many of her younger coworkers, she had not been trained to use word processors or personal computers and felt incompetent and apprehensive about the office automation project. Because of her lack of experience, she was reluctant to try out the new technology and stubbornly persisted in using the older machines and methods to do her job. She quickly became labeled as a "resister" who could not adjust to change. Thus, she fell victim to the self-fulfilling prophecy: She was not given the opportunity to train so that she could keep her skills up to date; she felt overwhelmed when the office automation systems were thrust on her; she continued to use her old methods as a result of her fear and anxiety; management blamed her "resistance" to change as a flaw in her character rather than as a result of their failure to provide her with opportunities to enhance her skills.

After studying such self-fulfilling prophecies, the U.S. Senate Special Committee on Aging (1982) concluded that age biases that are based on older workers' perceived resistance to change are unfounded. When viewed as more cautious and less willing to take risks, older and middle-age workers are less likely to be offered developmental opportunities, but without these opportunities, over a number of years they can lose motivation and become stagnant and less proficient. The committee called for a balance between the workers' obligations to keep up their skills and abilities to be productive and the companies' responsibilities to stimulate and provide opportunities for skill maintenance and growth. According to Rosow and Zager (1980) from the Work in America Institute, a research organization that studies such issues, it is time to discard the notion that people who have specialized for many years in one field or in one aspect of business lack the aptitudes, learning abilities, or skills to move to another.

Intellectual Performance and Age

In spite of the lack of supporting evidence, myths persist concerning age-related decrements in intellectual performance. Many still believe that intellectual changes parallel physical changes and that individuals reach their peak in their thirties and then deteriorate. Mental abilities, however, do not wane until individuals reach their early sixties, and even then, declines are not pronounced. After age sixty, there are some declines in *selected abilities* in *some individuals*, but clearly, middle-age to older adults are intellectually capable of being retrained.

One abilitiy that may change as individuals proceed through their sixties is memory for the names of objects and people. Older people do not forget uses of objects or pertinent facts about people but merely have more trouble naming them. It is important to keep in mind that the problem is not with memory per se but with the ability to name. This should not present unsurmountable obstacles for the older trainees because many jobs do not require this ability. On the other hand, performance in management or sales positions could suffer as a result of this deficit. Likewise, any training program that requires memorization of lists of names could be challenging for the trainee who has trouble naming. However, people can be taught methods for improving this naming ability if it is crucial to their succeeding in the retraining program and subsequently on the job. Program planners should consider including a module in the curriculum that would teach people techniques such as mediation imagery and mnemonics, which help people remember names. On the other hand, instructors should not require name memorization unless it will be essential for job performance. The transition committee should work closely with instructors to make this determination.

Learning to do a new job frequently does require acquiring new terminology, and older trainees can find this threatening. One way to help trainees with this problem is to distribute a booklet that defines technical terms and can be studied outside of the classroom. Instructors also should avoid using technical jargon at first because it can intimidate the older learner who is already anxious about being in an unfamiliar training environment. If these procedures are incorporated into the training program, the trainees' performance should not be hindered by any naming deficits that they may experience.

A second skill that shows some decrements in older workers is the ability to divide attention. Distractions become more detrimental as a person ages, but as individuals become aware of this change in themselves they can change their work habits to compensate. For example, they can learn to manage their time more efficiently so they can come closer to focusing on one task at a time. They also can organize their work environment to eliminate some common distractions.

As planners design the retraining program, they can provide a structure that alleviates the problem of distraction. First, the learning environment and the curriculum can be designed to allow attention to be focused on one task at a time. One way to accomplish this is to conduct the training away from the actual work area. In addition, curriculum subjects can be arranged in a sequence that allows learners to master one topic before moving on to another. To further aid students, the curriculum could include instruction on focusing attention and blocking distractions and also a module on time management so they could learn to avoid being pulled in several directions at once.

Getting Older Workers into Retraining Programs

Program planners should think about special issues pertaining to older workers at every stage in the development of the retraining program plan, but two issues demand focused attention from the outset. First, how will the company get older employees to apply to the programs, and second, what kind of selection process will be unbiased toward this age group?

Although we know that older workers are less likely to participate in retraining programs than are their younger colleagues, we do not know whether this is due to their lack of desire to retrain or due to biases in company policies and practices that discourage their participation. Work in America Institute has reported that, in some cases, managers may not want their senior employees to participate in retraining programs because they feel that they cannot spare these critical people. Top-level management can alleviate this situation by clarifying the importance of retraining even for senior employees and by establishing policies that guarantee that they are not excluded from programs.

As for lack of desire to retrain, middle-age and older adults become more willing to participate in educational and training programs as the "linear life pattern" changes (Rosow and Zager 1980). Traditionally, people have engaged in a sequence of prescribed activities at different times in their lives. For instance, people generally have been involved in education during the early years and through their teenage years. The education period generally has been followed by the work years, which extend until age sixty-five, at which time workers retire and engage in leisure activities, but this linear sequence is currently breaking down. People now are combining work, education, and leisure activities throughout their adult lives. Many college students combine their academic studies with work, and students frequently leave campus for a period of time to serve as interns or to fill co-op positions in their chosen professions. Likewise, many people continue to work at least part time past the age of sixty-five. If these trends continue, adults will become more willing to retrain and pursue educational and developmental opportunities so that their skills will not become obsolete. As people extend their work lives, companies can afford to invest in the training of middle-age and older workers because the payback will be greater.

After the program planners come up with strategies that encourage older employees to apply to retraining programs, they must design a selection process that will not be biased against those employees. Research has shown that middle-age and older people often do not perform as well on aptitude tests and other types of selection exams as do younger people (U.S. Senate Special Committee on Aging 1982), perhaps because of test anxiety or lack of recent experience in test taking. As in Leonard Martin's case, individuals without recent formal schooling may not be comfortable with formal testing, and although their actual aptitudes and abilities may equal their younger counterparts', those abilities may not be revealed through formal testing. Selection methods based on a functional analysis of past work history are much better indicators of the applicants' aptitudes and abilities. These methods look at the individual's demonstrated level of expertise in a variety of types of skills, such as the kinds of abilities required by each of the employee's previous jobs. The analysis would consider all kinds of skills—including analyzing, computing, coaching, precision working, and so forth.

The case of Marjory Ware can illustrate this type of selection method. Marjory was forty-five years old when she applied to a computer programming retraining program. She had worked in a variety of manufacturing departments over the years and most recently had served as a department technician in charge of working on high-priority jobs. She had been in charge of making sure that everyone had work, monitoring the progress of work within the department, and generally providing the manager with status reports. When she applied to the retraining program, she feared that she would have to take aptitude tests. She had not been tested for years and was anxious over whether she would perform well. Instead of testing, the selection committee performed a functional job analysis on her past positions and looked at how well she had performed each function uncovered by the analysis. They found that she had demonstrated a high level of competence in skills such as coordinating, monitoring, analyzing, and problem solving and had proven that she was logical and methodical with her work. On the basis of this functional job analysis, the selection committee decided that Marjory's proven abilities made her a strong candidate for retraining.

Although it is a little more complicated to administer, this type of job analysis offers a fair method for assessing worker interests and skills with respect to the requirements for the new career. After all, older employees' experiences are often their most valuable credentials. This approach to selecting trainees is likely to be fairer to older employees. In spite of the complexity of this system, the results can be useful not only for selecting candidates but also for determining the content of the training and curriculum.

For instance, although the functional job analysis indicated that Marjory had many aptitudes that would be required for computer programming, she did not have much experience in communicating with a mix of professional people. As a programmer, she would be working with individuals from a variety of different areas with an assortment of backgrounds. In fact, many of the applicants chosen for the retraining lacked this background, so the functional job analyses led to the inclusion of a module in the curriculum that addressed how to work with people from various areas in the company.

In summary, as the importance of ensuring that existing employees have the right skills increases, establishing fair selection procedures also grows more significant. Company leaders must be sure to clearly establish their desire to include senior employees in training programs and develop strategies for encouraging individuals in this age group to participate in retraining programs. Program planners also must devise selection methods that are not biased against older candidates. This usually means finding alternatives to the traditional testing approach to selection.

Older Learners in the Classroom

Almost all participants in retraining programs are older than traditional students. Although they will not have greater difficulties learning, the conditions under which they learn best deviate from those found in the traditional classroom. Malcolm S. Knowles (1984), considered by many to be the foremost authority in the field of adult education, discusses the following three distinguishing characteristics of adult learners:

1. *The adult learner is self-directing rather than dependent on the teacher.* When people mature into adulthood, they become responsible for their own lives, but adults too frequently assume a role of dependency in the classroom due to earlier conditioning. They "demand to be taught." If this reliance is perpetuated by the instructor, the adult learners are likely to become resentful because they are not used to feeling helpless in other facets of their lives. The adult educational program should be structured for self-directed learning. Older trainees are especially likely to respond negatively to being treated like dependent, experienceless children.

Jack Lord, for example, a forty-eight-year-old participant in a retraining program, complained that one of the instructors was disturbingly patronizing even though he was only half Jack's age. The instructor came from the local community college where he was used to working with the eighteen- to twenty-one-year-old age group. He attempted to follow the same method with the retraining program that he used in his more traditional classroom. He followed a highly structured format and did not encourage questioning or discussion. In fact, on one occasion when Jack asked a question concerning how the lecture material applied to a situation with which he was familiar, the instructor accused him of trying to change the focus of the lecture. Jack reacted adversely to this accusation and began regularly asking questions that challenged the instructor. The instructor, in turn, charged Jack with harassing him, and the struggle between the two continued throughout the duration of the class. The power struggle between Jack and the instructor became so disruptive that other students were unable to learn. Finally, another student went to the program manager and described the problem, and the program manager intervened to work out the problems between the two.

2. *Adult learners have a great variety of experiences on which to build learning.* Because they bring varied and rich experiences with them to the educational situation, older learners frequently can learn from each other. Instructors should provide opportunities for adult students to engage in discussion. Perhaps instructors can design some tasks to be completed in small groups, and the group can determine how to carry out the assignment. This technique allows students to discuss the material with each other and provides an opportunity for some self-direction. Furthermore, the group assign-

ment can facilitate the building of rapport by eliminating the barriers of age and status. Still another positive effect of this approach is that it allows time for trainees to develop some self-confidence before they are evaluated individually (Mintz 1986). The group assignment also provides the trainees with valuable practice in working with others. Another effective method for teaching adults with varied experiences is to individualize training. Because of their heterogeneous backgrounds, their learning needs are likely to be diverse. The individualized approach allows for the material to build on their varying backgrounds.

3. *Adults are internally motivated to learn and seek out education to fulfill needs in their lives. Their orientation to learning is problem-centered.* If trainees are to maintain a high level of motivation throughout the training, they must be convinced that they need to know the material that the instructors present. In this respect, they differ from traditional students, who are more likely to be motivated by external forces, such as pressure from parents. Because adult retrainees are likely to be driven by internal needs, they must be able to relate what they are learning to the job that they will be performing. In the case of Jack Lord, the instructor's reluctance to address Jack's questions about how the information fit with his experiences in his work led to an escalating antagonism. The problem probably could have been avoided if the instructor had been more aware of the differences between adults and younger students in their approaches to learning.

Another excellent way to assist trainees in linking their studies to the job is to arrange at the end of training for them to visit the areas in which they will be working. They can talk with people who are already in the positions for which they are preparing and thus can get a better sense of how the information their instructors present applies to their work.

Because adults are problem-centered in their motivation to learn, the optimal learning environment is one in which the material is organized logically. These conditions are especially important for older workers. Although they generally do well with formal reasoning and with perceiving relationships, some older learners tend to experience difficulties remembering abstract and disconnected material (Franz 1983, Managing an Aging Workforce Conference 1982). For the most part, adults learn best when training tasks are simplified yet whole rather than broken down into disconnected units (Belbin and Belbin 1972), an approach that makes it easier for them to relate their training to their jobs. Instruction should help older trainees conceptualize how the new skills and information fit together and how new concepts connect to things they already know or to previous experiences.

Although these teaching strategies are particularly useful for instructing middle-age and older trainees, they can help learners of any age retain information. The logical and organized presentation of the material accompanied by methods that help the students relate the facts to their own experiences can enhance comprehension for everyone.

Undoubtedly one of the most important factors in determining whether adult students will succeed in a training program is the degree to which they can control their anxiety. Sometimes their fear of making mistakes can reach such high levels that they cannot learn. Students may become paralyzed by fear and incapable of performing in the classroom or completing assignments. In some cases, the older trainees may have been managers or executives whose positions have been eliminated due to company restructuring. They may feel particularly threatened by being in what they perceive to be the subordinate position of a trainee. For example, Sally Rosenthal had been manager in a department that was being phased out altogether due to a company merger and found herself in a retraining program with some of the individuals who previously had been under her supervision. She was in the peculiar position of not just working with them as equals but of actually feeling inferior because she had been away from a training environment longer them most of them. She was understandably fearful of appearing incompetent in her new role as a student and also was afraid that other students might not accept her because several of them had worked for her. The program manager and the instructors were aware of the circumstances and were able to alleviate some of her discomfort by the way they structured the classroom. They organized activities at the beginning of the program that were designed to help the trainees get to know each other and to learn to work together. They also used the group assignment method at first to allow rapport to build and to minimize the anxiety that comes from being evaluated individually. They were sensitive to any early signs of potential problems so that they could act quickly to prevent them. Through these efforts, they succeeded in creating an atmosphere that was not extremely stressful and thereby increased the probabilities of the trainees' success.

Even though older adults are likely to be anxious about retraining, their chances of succeeding in a program are great if their uneasiness can be alleviated. In fact, the learning conditions under which older adults are likely to feel most at ease are those in which they are being retrained by their employers for new positions within the company. The trainees get support from their fellow trainees, with whom they are frequently acquainted before the training, and gain confidence from a familiar environment if the retraining is conducted on site. In addition, trainees are likely to believe that the company's willingness to retrain them signifies a belief in their abilities and value to the company. The company that invests in retraining its older employees is clearly making a commitment to their continued employment—a fact that bolsters trainees' confidence.

Of course, planners can design the program to minimize the anxiety of all learners, including older ones. First, the program can begin with tasks and activities that are not the most critical for success in the profession and are not too physically or mentally demanding. For example, during an orientation module trainees can learn more about the profession or job for which they are training and can be introduced to people with similar backgrounds who have already made the career transition. Exposure to others who have succeeded can inspire confidence.

Furthermore, the program can be designed to minimize trainees' fears of making mistakes. At the beginning of the program, trainees should be given plenty of nonevaluative feedback about their performance and the opportunity to catch their own mistakes in the early stages of the program. Moreover, the early courses can be designed for self-paced learning so that the trainees do not feel a lot of time pressure. Although initially the training should be structured so that accuracy is emphasized over speed, it is possible that the older trainee might become obsessed with avoiding mistakes.

This kind of preoccupation frequently stems from the fear of failure—one of the most destructive types of anxiety. Instructors should discourage obsessions with accuracy that get in the way of completing tasks. One way to ease this type of fear is to eliminate the traditional methods for evaluating students, such as final exams; major examinations can be overwhelming to older students. If tests are used, they should be administered frequently, so that students get regular feedback, and should match the requirements of the profession as closely as possible. If the trainee never will have to recall technical information from memory when on the job, it probably is not necessary to test for this ability. On the other hand, testing for understanding and applying that technical information would be appropriate.

The instructors, retraining program manager, and others associated with retraining can help build confidence in trainees by emphasizing that they all have a stake in the success of each trainee. If the selection process was conducted carefully, after all, all who participate in the retraining program should be able to complete the training. Those who were judged incapable of succeeding were not chosen in the first place.

In addition to noting the attitudinal and motivational needs of the adult student, instructors should work around any potential physical limitations of older trainees. For example, they should avoid overhead projectors and small screens because older trainees may not be able to see information presented from a distance through these media and can accommodate for hearing impairments through seating arrangements. Of course, arranging to work around any potential physical limitations of older trainees requires tact. Although it is important for instructors to be sensitive to special needs of older students, it is crucial for these students to feel no stigma as a result. If there is a large age discrepancy among trainees, older trainees are likely to feel somewhat threatened by younger ones. The program manager and the instructors need to set up an environment that is optimal for learning without singling out older students as being disadvantaged.

In general, instructors merely need to be alert to ways in which they can facilitate the older adults' learning processes. Adults differ from younger, traditional students in their motivations and learning styles, but retraining programs generally can be easily tailored to the requirements of older adults.

Older Adults in Transition

In addition to the unfounded yet persistent beliefs that older employees are not capable of learning, some company leaders worry about whether older workers will be able to handle the changes that accompany retraining. Large numbers of employers perceive older workers as less flexible and more resistant to change than their younger colleagues. Although the perception that older workers resist change is widespread, there is no evidence that age per se has anything to do with adaptability. Individuals in every age group vary in their abilities to deal with change. Of course, people of all ages form attachments to their environments, including ideas, people, and companies. Because they have been around longer, older workers are likely to have formed stronger attachments to their circumstances than have their younger counterparts, and changes therefore may have a greater effect on older workers (Winstanley and Sheppard 1982). However, this does not mean that older employees are necessarily more likely than younger ones to resist change.

The change process requires people of any age to unhook from the past before they can fully embrace the present and the future. This unhooking from past attachments often requires a period of grief, and during this time, people are likely to experience and express some anxiety and loss. Sometimes observers confuse these indications of grief with signs of resistance. On the contrary, this distress is a natural part of the change process and does not mean that the change is being fought. Those in transition are merely going through a necessary step that will prepare them to accept and adapt to the new circumstances. Older workers may show stronger signs of grief because they are unhooking from attachments that were longer in the making. Company leaders should not confuse their behavior with resistance.

Even though older workers are no more likely to oppose change than are younger workers, they may experience changes in their personalities that influence how they respond to transitions. Research on adult development and life phases does indicate that motivation, values, and personal style frequently shift as people age. Older adults tend to become more reflective as well as more likely to examine the possible consequences of their actions. Although people gain in overall effectiveness, competence, and self-control as they age, they are less likely to test their limits (Winstanley and Sheppard 1982). They tend to feel less vulnerable and have less need for manipulating or controlling relationships. They tend to withdraw from involvements that are not rewarding, including relationships with people as well as engagement in tasks (Franz, 1983). Men seem to become more nurturant and affiliative as they reach the older years, shifting from emphasis on career to emphasis on relationships (Levinson et al. 1978; Gould 1978; Franz 1983). Women, on the other hand, tend to become more self-confident, more assertive, less dependent, and more instrumental (Lowenthal et al. 1975). Adults do change as they age, but the important question is how age affects reactions to transitions.

As personal satisfaction and affiliative needs grow increasingly important, training and career transitions may become more difficult. If these transitions disrupt relationships such as friendship or family ties, older workers may have trouble adjusting. On the other hand, since workers tend to feel less vulnerable and more self-controlled as they age, older workers may be better prepared to cope with the stress that accompanies transitions. Therefore, it is difficult to assess exactly how the older worker will handle career changes. Research indicates that older adults' responses to transitions tend to depend on the degree to which events are predictable (Neugarten 1970). Changes that violate their expectations seem to be more upsetting than foreseeable circumstances. Therefore, if they view job change and retraining as normal processes for employees at all points in their work lives, older adults are not likely to respond negatively. On the other hand, if the company usually restricts job change and retraining to younger workers, older workers may show signs of distress if the company suddenly shifts and expects them to make these transitions. The way the company *normally* handles the training and development of older workers necessarily influences the nature of reaction to a retraining transition.

Summary and Implication

Companies are becoming increasingly dependent on their older workers as the demographic characteristics of the workforce change. Indeed, the experience, maturity, and loyalty of middle-age to older employees make them valuable assets to companies that develop practices that allow for their continued productivity. Because many people within this older age group need to update their skills, retraining program planners should pay special attention to conditions that are conducive to their learning and making successful transitions.

Intellectual capabilities do not decrease in people in their fifties, sixties, and seventies. In fact, vocabulary, comprehension, and math abilities change very little with age. If sudden changes in these capabilities do occur, the cause is likely to be disease, not age per se, and some medical disorders that do not affect intellectual performance in younger people may affect these abilities in older persons. The two cognitive abilities that occasionally decline in people over the age of sixty are the capacities to remember names and to divide attention. Nevertheless, people can be taught techniques that help them compensate for any decrements experienced in these abilities. Likewise, learning environments can be structured to assist older trainees with these potential problems.

Attitudinal and motivational factors seem to have a major effect on older adults' acquisition of new information. Indeed, the anxiety that older adults may experience as they face a learning environment is more likely to lead to failure than are decrements in intellectual functioning. Some educators claim that older adults are likely to experience more stress in training situations and that their performance is more likely to be affected by the stress (Belbin and Belbin 1972). Although there is no solid evidence that they experience more training-related stress, we know that older learners tend to be self-conscious and fear the embarrassment that would accompany their making mistakes. The aggravating factor is that older persons who enter retraining programs have been in jobs for years in which they felt very competent and rarely made mistakes. In many cases they were role models for younger employees, who looked to them for guidance. Many find it difficult and distasteful to be dependent again and to feel helpless and incompetent. For all of these reasons it is important for program planners and instructors to be aware of the special needs of the adult learner. For example, the program should be structured for self-directed learning as much as possible so that helpless, dependent feelings are alleviated. Furthermore, the educational process should include methods for tapping into and building on the rich experiences that these senior employees bring with them to the classroom.

Finally, although older employees are no more likely to resist change than are younger people, their responses to transitions may vary from their younger colleagues under some circumstances. First, because their attachments to their jobs and to the work environment are likely to be stronger, the loss and grief that they experience through the transition process may also be greater. On the other hand, the feelings of self-control and competence that increase with age may prepare them to deal with transitions better than they could have in their earlier years. The degree to which they accept the transition is likely to depend on how predictable the retraining demands were for them. Furthermore, their interest and involvement in the retraining is likely to depend heavily on how clearly they can see a correlation between the training and a rewarding job.

Of course, the way in which the program is designed will certainly affect the ease with which older adults make a job transition. Planners can develop program details that allow trainees to have some sense of control and self-direction. In addition, program planners and instructors should promote activities and actions aimed at building cohesiveness and rapport within the group of students so that their relationship needs are met. Finally, those involved in implementing the retraining program should realize that a period of breaking away from attachments to the past is to be expected, especially with older workers. A certain amount of anxiety and grief are inevitable. This does not mean that trainees are going to resist changes or that they will fail in making the transitions required by the retraining process. After all, as William Bridges (1980) puts it in his book *Transitions: Making Sense of Life's Changes*, transitions begin with endings.

References

Barton, P. 1982. *Worklife Transitions*. New York: McGraw-Hill.

Belbin, E., and P. M. Belbin. 1972. *Problems in Adult Retraining*. London: Heinemann.

Bridges, W. 1980. *Transition: Making Sense of Life's Changes*. Reading, Mass.: Addison-Wesley.

Cohn, R. M. March 1979. "Age and Satisfactions from Work." *Journal of Gerontology*.

Franz, J. B. Sept.–Dec. Vol. 9, No. 5–6, 1983. "Cognitive Development and Career Retraining in Older Adults." *Educational Gerontology*.

Gould, R. 1978. *Transformations*. New York: Simon & Schuster.

Harris L., et al. 1981. *Aging in the Eighties: America in Transition*. Washington, D.C.: National Council on Aging.

Kaminski, V. 1983. "Designing a Seminar for Managers of Older Workers." *Training and Development Journal* (July).

Knowles, M. S. 1984. *Andragogy in Action*. San Francisco: Jossey-Bass.

Levinson, D. J., C. M. Darrow, E. B. Klein, et al. 1978. *Seasons of a Man's Life*. New York: Alfred A. Knopf.

Lowenthal, M. F., M. Thurnher, D. Chiriboga, and associates. 1975. *Four Stages of Life: A Comparative Study of Women and Men Facing Transitions*. San Francisco: Jossey-Bass.

Managing an Aging Workforce Conference. 1982. *Business Issues in America*. Papers presented at the Travelers Insurance Company Conference, New York, February.

Mintz, F. 1986. "Retraining: The Graying of the Training Room." *Personnel* (October).

Neugarten, B. L. Fall, Vol. IV No. 1, 1970. "Dynamics of the Transition to Old Age." *Journal of Geriatric Psychiatry*.

Rosow, J., and R. Zager. 1980. *The Future of Older Workers in America*. Scarsdale, N.Y.: Work in America Policy Study Institute.

U.S. Senate Special Committee on Aging. 1982. *Aging and the Work Force: Human Resources Strategies*. Washington, D.C.: USGPO.

Winstanley, N. B., and H. L. Sheppard. 1982. "How Does Aging Affect Job Performance—and Performance Appraisals?" Paper presented as part of the *Business Issues in an Aging America Report* at the Travelers Insurance Company Conference, February.

CHAPTER EIGHT

◆

Summary and Conclusions

THE WORLD of work is changing swiftly and dramatically as companies of all sizes and types experience the pressures of turbulent times. New technologies, increased competition from international markets, deregulation, and shifts in the basis of our national and international economies are only a few of the major challenges facing American businesses and industries. As corporations transform their goals and strategies, they also affect the very nature of work. Their strategic plans must include provisions for redirecting people to operate effectively within the new work environment.

By the beginning of the next century, a mere eleven years from now, millions of jobs in both the manufacturing and service sectors will have been restructured and, as a result, will require a new mix of skills. Furthermore, as many occupations become obsolete and fade from existence, changing technologies and changing economies will generate millions of new jobs and occupations. These new positions created in the "information age" will require higher levels of skills than the old jobs left behind with the "industrial age." Thus, American businesses face a potential mismatch between the skills that will be available in the workforce and the skills that will be required for the workplace. Because people who do not have the right skills cannot do their jobs, companies face the threats of lowered productivity and manpower shortages. At the same time, American workers are subject to the trauma of displacement and unemployment.

In order to prevent these potentially catastrophic occurrences, companies need to develop long-term personnel and training plans that coordinate with their overall strategies for the future. In a recent book concerning human resource development planning, Nadler and Wiggs (1986:213) argue that companies frequently offer training programs that are currently popular but not necessary in light of the company's goals. Human resource development planning today must be responsive to "the constantly evolving and fluid nature of the organization's business" that results from competition, changes in technology, markets, and products or services.

The establishment of private-sector retraining programs often can prevent the damaging effects of a serious skill mismatch within a company. The most successful programs are those that equip trainees with skills for performing different jobs within the same company. These retraining programs differ from a company's routine training activities in that they prepare employees for significantly different jobs or careers. In fact, in many cases the retraining requires participants to make a radical transition from the old job to the new. Compared to more traditional training programs, retraining projects generally include much more than simple instruction for the acquisition of a limited set of new skills. Instead, retraining often requires a socialization process that leads to new attitudes, values, and assumptions about the relationship between the individual and work. This book has examined several key themes in addressing the challenge of this retraining process.

Basic Skill Deficiencies Block Retraining

The changing requirements in the workplace pose serious challenges for retraining. Although no one knows the exact skill specifications that will be required by future jobs, we do know that almost everyone will need a strong foundation in the basic skills of reading, mathematics, reasoning, and communicating. Many of our workers, however, lack an acceptable level of proficiency in these basics. American businesses already experience problems with productivity as a result of employees' deficiencies in reading, math, and reasoning, but people who enter the workforce in the next decade are likely to be even less adept in these fundamental skills. Moreover, the lack of basic skills is limiting the job advancement of today's employees, a predicament that will worsen as workplace

Summary and Conclusions

requirements continue to evolve. Currently, approximately 30 million Americans are functionally illiterate, and even more alarming, the growth rate in illiteracy is approximately 2.3 million a year. The National Center for Education Statistics reports that if this trend continues, approximately 2 million people graduating from high school in 1990 will be unqualified for any type of job (Choate and Linger 1986).

The skill deficiencies of the current workforce are especially alarming in light of the trends for the future. Employees who lack fundamental skills cannot advance and are extremely vulnerable to skill obsolescence and possible unemployment. Growing numbers of companies are facing this problem as they attempt to modernize their technologies and procedures. If employees cannot read and write, they will not be trainable. From the standpoint of the corporation, these deficiencies will affect general productivity, product quality, worker safety, and the amount of required management or supervision time. As a result of these massive deficiencies in basic skills, remedial education is of growing importance to corporations.

Employers Vary in Their Commitment to Training

American businesses are committed to training their employees. The formal corporate education industry is currently a $30 billion enterprise, and businesses spend $180 billion on informal employee training. As many as 40 million workers a year now receive training provided by their employers. On the other hand, in spite of these impressive numbers, all employees do not have equal access to these training opportunities. Although managers and professionals are the most likely to participate in retraining, skill obsolescence is not limited to the white-collar professions. Indeed, blue-collar workers are at least as vulnerable as are their white-collar colleagues. Moreover, the large companies are responsible for a high percentage of training.

Although training is a high priority in corporate America, retraining is not. Companies still prefer to hire new employees rather than retrain existing employees as positions open up. This is likely to change. When businesses experience problems in finding people to hire for their vacant positions, the company leaders are likely to increase their commitment to retraining.

Employers Vary in Their Commitment to Training

Most companies still prefer to conduct their own training in-house for their employees. Many have expressed a reluctance to collaborate with educational institutions or government agencies in these endeavors and feel that these organizations do not understand their businesses. In addition, they object to what they perceive to be the overwhelming amounts of paperwork that government often requires. In spite of these arguments, collaborative ventures are likely to become more acceptable as the need for retraining increases dramatically. Businesses are likely to find that they cannot keep up with the accelerating demand for new workers. Companies are likely to be more willing to work in partnership with other organizations in order to handle the enormous training loads that they will face.

Some exemplary partnerships for retraining are already in place. These collaborative projects vary tremendously in nature and in scope. For example, some of the currently existing business-education partnerships focus on companies assisting in the long-term improvement of the public schools so that the community or region will have a pool of skilled graduates in the labor force. In other partnerships businesses become clients of educational institutions. Many educational institutions are currently contracting with businesses to provide training for their employees, either through programs where instructors go to the company to train or where employees attend classes on the school's campus.

Critics of these business-education partnerships argue that collaborative arrangements are not practical, pointing to problems such as the lack of a shared language between these two different types of organizations. Furthermore, they voice concerns for what they view as the lack of coordination and focus in these partnerships. On the other hand, proponents of joint efforts claim that partnerships are optimal for retraining. Although businesses are in the best position to identify their training needs, professional educators and trainers have the skills to design the curriculum and administer the instruction.

The key to whether a partnership succeeds or fails, however, lies in the qualifications of the individuals who represent both partners. The people who represent the business in the partnership should have some understanding of the educational process, and the educators who provide the training should have demonstrated their

Summary and Conclusions

abilities to teach adults and to direct their instruction to practical business applications. Despite the competence of instructors and other individuals representing the educational institution, however, the company must be actively involved in all phases of the retraining, including planning, development, implementation, and evaluation.

Training and Long-Range Planning: The Strategic Link

Effective retraining matches programs to the company's plans for the future. If the human resource development personnel create their own plans independently of top-level decision makers, their efforts are likely to be ineffective. Frequently a company's training department focuses on what other companies are doing or adopts programs and approaches that trade magazines and organizations are promoting. This approach to designing training programs usually wastes time and money. Although participants may enjoy attending classes that cover trendy topics, the skills and knowledge that they acquire are likely to be useless in increasing their effectiveness on the job unless the topics are tied to identified company needs.

The process of making long-term projections of employee and skill needs may be inexact, but most business plans suffer from the same imprecision. Nevertheless, just as the projections that go into strategic business plans are indispensable if the company is to remain competitive, personnel estimates are equally critical to the company's future.

Although most companies project their personnel needs to some degree, those estimates generally are limited to a few months into the future. Hiring and training policies should be based on what the company will be like five to ten years ahead in order to affect whether the company's workforce will be productive and thus whether the business will survive. In the highly competitive national and world economies, no company can afford to run the risk of experiencing a shortage of critical skills.

The personnel projections that are crucial to companies today need more than a rough estimate of the numbers of people who will be needed in the array of occupations currently existing in the organization, however. The essential piece in the strategic personnel plan is identification of the skills and knowledge that employees must possess to perform the predicted array of jobs. Changing technologies and organizational practices affect the kinds of occupations that are crucial for doing business as well as the required knowledge base and the mix of skills needed to effectively function within these occupations. This need for employees with the right skills is so critical to companies that they should not blindly depend on finding appropriately prepared people to hire. Educational and training institutions frequently lag behind industry in their understanding of what is required by the workplace, so that the training that their students receive is often outdated by the time that they graduate. The private sector can help solve this problem by projecting their skill needs and communicating this information to the education and training communities. Even if the schools adequately prepare students, however, the decline of young people in the population means that there will be fewer and fewer entrants into the labor force. Companies will need to build innovative strategies for maintaining an adequately skilled workforce.

The personnel plan should build on the skill projections derived from the current supply. Businesses need to develop a picture of their workers in terms of technical, cognitive, interpersonal, and self-management skills. If current employees do not have the mix of abilities that skill projections indicate will be needed, employers will have a data base on which to build training and hiring strategies. Companies should not make quick decisions about how to solve any skill mismatch projections that the analyses uncover, but, instead, should generate a list of alternatives and compare the costs and benefits of each potential solution. The commonly held assumption that the cheapest solution is to fire and hire may be cost effective under some circumstances, but at other times it may be very expensive in terms of both actual dollars as well as morale, loyalty, and productivity.

Successful Retraining Requires Careful Planning

If the company chooses retraining as one solution to the skill mismatch dilemma, the leaders must carefully plan the retraining strategy. The lack of thoughtful preparation can lead to disastrous results and wasted money. For medium to large firms, the best approach is

Summary and Conclusions

to establish a team of people that represent a range of departments within the company. The composition of the team depends on the scale of the retraining, but in general personnel, education, communications, and any labor unions functioning within the organization should contribute members to the planning team. The role that is most crucial to the entire retraining process is that of the program manager. Having the same individual serve in the position from the very beginning of the planning until the training is completed and the trainees are working in their new jobs provides the program with continuity. Although the program manager has many responsibilities, among the most important is serving as counselor to and advocate for trainees. Because of the stress generated by the programs, participants need someone who will support them and to whom they can turn if they have problems. The program manager must be able to relate to the personal needs of the trainees as well as coordinate all of the activities pertaining to planning, implementing, and evaluating the program.

Every member of the planning team should be familiar with the decisions that lead up to the program. Because the group is responsible for drawing up a blueprint based on the original business rationale for retraining, it must understand how and why the company leaders chose retraining rather than other options for dealing with skill imbalances. The retraining process is too expensive to risk overlooking the specifics of how it will meet the identified need. Therefore, every team member must have a clear understanding of the program's mission, goals, and objectives, and all of their planning should be done within the context of this background information.

The components of the blueprint or retraining program plan are interrelated. For example, all of the decisions concerning every aspect of the program depend on the budget and the time frame for the retraining process. Likewise, the curriculum and the level at which courses will be taught must be linked to the characteristics that the selection committee looks for in trainees chosen for the program. The committee members must consider these issues simultaneously if they are to plan a program that can realistically accomplish its goals. Companies that attempt to teach classes at a level considerably beyond the capabilities of the students selected for the program are likely to find that their efforts are wasted or that to accomplish their goals they must expand the budget and lengthen the training period beyond their original plans. These unfortunate circumstances can be avoided if the committee considers the interdependencies among all of the components of the program and completes its planning before beginning any phase of the retraining process.

One of the most important tasks facing the retraining team is to devise a plan for announcing and publicizing the program. These initial messages concerning the retraining can affect the way people throughout the organization react to subsequent steps in the retraining process. The communications plan should emphasize that retraining is a positive step for the company to take and that the entire process is the result of careful analysis and planning. If the process is to be welcomed by employees and retain its credibility, no program details should appear to have been neglected or haphazardly devised. The committee also must be prepared to respond to the local press or other community groups that indicate an interest in the program. If the retraining is on a large scale, people outside of the company may wonder whether trainees will move elsewhere after completing the training. Likewise, community leaders are also likely to wonder whether the retraining might be a sign of other major changes in the company that might affect the local region. The retraining team should establish how they will address these issues.

Keeping Up with Change

The need for retraining indicates large-scale and widespread changes in the workplace and should not be treated as an isolated event. Policy makers must examine the broad picture of transition within the company, first, by analyzing how impending changes probably will affect people throughout the company. Using this analysis as the foundation for their decisions, they can develop plans to enhance the positive effects of retraining and either eliminate or minimize the negative effects of the planned changes.

One of the most significant contributions that a firm can make to its employees is to create an environment that not only permits but encourages continuous career growth and development. The companies that survive major changes into the next decade will

Summary and Conclusions

make the commitment to foster the growth and development of their employees of all ages. Although the major responsibility for keeping up with change rests with each individual, no one can devise an effective strategy for keeping abreast of change without some knowledge of the company's plans for the future. If employees are aware of circumstances that might affect their jobs, they will be able to avoid skill obsolescence.

In addition to furnishing information, managers can assist employees to assess their skills and devise plans for self-development. Managers can be especially helpful in advising employees about training and retraining options and about setting priorities and exploring career and training alternatives.

Retraining Can Be Stressful

Retraining programs are demanding and therefore usually stressful for the participants. The pressure of the training itself coupled with the tension of career transition can be overwhelming for trainees, and yet participants need to be at their best if they are to succeed in the program. All those involved in planning and administering the retraining program should be aware of the special issues surrounding the transition and should consider ways to prevent the potential stress from becoming debilitating. Some program planners provide for a counselor to work with the trainees throughout the entire transitional period, while others ensure that instructors and others who work with trainees are prepared to assist with their anxieties. Although the company can provide support and guidance to the trainees, ultimately each individual must devise a personal strategy for dealing with the pressures that accompany the changes. Program administrators should encourage them to face the experience thoughtfully and realistically.

It Is Never Too Late to Retrain

Research evidence indicates that companies depend increasingly on older employees. Because senior members of the organization will need to update or even learn completely new skills, program planners should strive to create the conditions that are conducive to their successful retraining.

Although older employees are as capable intellectually as are their younger counterparts, the two age groups may not approach the experience of retraining in quite the same way. Attitudinal and motivational factors have a major effect on older adults' performance in a training environment. They need to have a sense of control over their learning. Indeed, because they are used to performing their jobs competently, older adults find it especially distasteful to feel helpless and dependent in the classroom. Instructors can anticipate and avoid problems by structuring the training to be somewhat self-directed and to draw on the experiences of trainees.

Older adults are no more likely to resist change than are younger people, but they are likely to have formed stronger attachments to the jobs, occupations, and colleagues that they are leaving behind. They therefore may experience more grief as they disconnect from the past. This disengagement is natural and, in fact, is a necessary part of the transitional process and should not be confused with resistance or lack of acceptance of change.

Conclusions

The task of maintaining a competent and skilled workforce in our nation is enormous. The challenge is of such magnitude that no one sector within our country can tackle the entire training burden. Corporate America must share with government and the educational community the task of retraining. If our businesses and industries are to survive and thrive throughout the remainder of this century and into the next, the responsibility to retrain must become a top priority within the private sector and move from its peripheral status within companies to a central position in strategic and long-range planning processes. Corporate leaders must understand that to achieve their carefully constructed strategic goals they need workers who have the skills to effectively implement those strategies. As the pool of qualified entrants into the workforce shrinks, retraining will become the key to increased productivity in the twenty-first century.

Summary and Conclusions

References

Choate, P., and J. Linger. 1986. *The High-Flex Society.* New York: Alfred A. Knopf.

Nadler, L., and G. D. Wiggs. 1986. *Managing Human Resource Development.* San Francisco: Jossey-Bass.

Index

Administration on Aging, 125
Age Discrimination in Employment Act, 125
Apprenticeships, 119
AT&T, 5, 12, 50
Automation, 22
  effect on managers, 15–17
  in offices, 10–11

Banks and financial institutions, technical skills requirements in, 23
Barton, Paul, 128
Basic skills, 3, 30–32, 52, 145–46
  remedial education for, 35–42
Basic Skills Enhancement Program (BSEP), 49–50
Basic Skills in the U.S. Workforce, 31
Beyond Mechanization (Hirschhorn), 25
Blue-collar workers, skill shifts, facing, 1, 2, 146
Bowles, Richard, 104
Bridges, William, 116, 142
Budget and time frame, for retraining programs, 82–83
Bureau of Labor Statistics, 12
Business rationale statement, retraining program plans, 74

California, state-local governmental retraining programs, 46
Career planning, 99–107, 120
  self-assessment, 101–7
Carl Perkins Vocational Education Act, 44
Caterpillar company, 55
Center for Public Resources, 31
Clark, Donald, 50
Collaborative work environments, 19–21
Communications departments, corporate, role in retraining, 7, 89–92, 98, 151

Communications member, retraining program team, 70(table), 71
Communications Workers of America, 5, 50
Community Work Site Education and Training program, California, 46
Companies, preparing for change in, 107–10
  analysis of impact, 108–9
  development of action plan, 109–10
Computer-integrated manufacturing systems (CIM), 19
Computers and computer literacy, 28. *See also* Automation; Microprocessor technology
Congressional Office of Technology Assessment, 2, 9, 17
Corporate commitment to retraining, 146–48
Corporate culture, role of, and technological innovation, 28–30
Corporate departments involved in retraining, 7–8
Corporate goals and retraining, 54–67, 148–49
  assessing demand by projecting skill requirements, 59–61
  assessing supply by identifying employees' skills, 61–62
  checking for imbalances, 63–64
  cost-benefit comparisons of retraining vs. firing, 64–66
  long-term vs. short-term personnel plans, 56–59
  reasons for, 54–55
  soliciting input from top management, 55–56
  summary and implications, 67
Curriculum plan, retraining programs, 83–89
  components, 83–85
  course objectives and content, 85

Index

Curriculum plan *(cont.)*
    measurement methods, 85–87
    more considerations on, 88–89
    teaching methods, 87–88
Customized Job Training for Business and Industry (Kopecek), 51

Displaced workers, 2–4
    characteristics of, 9–11

Economy, structural changes in, 1–5, 11–14
Educational institutions, cooperative retraining programs with business, 48, 49–51
Education and training departments, corporate, involved in retraining, 7
Education member, retraining program teams, 70(table), 71
Employee Development and Training Program (EDTP), 47–48, 50
Employee involvement programs, 18–21
Employment Training Panel, California, 46
Entry skills, 84
Evaluation
    of retraining programs, 94–96
        achieving business goals, 95
        long-range effectiveness, 95–96
        training effectiveness, 94–95
    of trainees' learning, 85–87

Family and friends, effect of, on participants in retraining, 114–16
Fear of failure in retraining programs, 113, 137
Firing/hiring vs. retraining, cost-benefit analysis, 64–66
Ford Motor Company
    basic skills training at, 42
    employee involvement programs at, 18, 20
    UAW cooperative program with, 47–48, 49–50
Functional planning, 54–55
Future Shock (Toffler), 23

General Electric, 49

General Motors
    basic skills training at, 42
    employee involvement programs at, 18
Ginzberg, Eli, 13
Goals and objectives, retraining program plans, 74
Government, involvement in retraining programs, 7, 44–47
    federal programs, 44–45
    state and local programs, 44, 45–47
Greater Cincinnati Industrial Training Corporation, 49

Health care, 24, 29
Hirschhorn, Larry, 25
Hughes Aircraft, 46
Human Resource Implications of Robotics, 58
Human resource planning
    failure to prioritize, 4–5
    forecasting corporate needs, 56–64
    linking to corporate strategic mission, 5

IBM Corporation, 12, 50
Implementation of retraining programs, 92–94
    monitoring instruction, 93
    providing feedback, 93
    tracking reactions, 93–94
Information/knowledge-based businesses, 13, 19
Intellectual performance and age of worker, 129–30, 141

Job analysis, assessing demand for skill requirements through, 59–60
Job characteristics and job satisfaction, 102–3
Job design and skills requirement, 18–21
Job placement, following retraining program, 81–82, 97–98
Job Training and Partnership Act (JTPA), 4, 44–45

Ketchum, Lyman, 27
Kopecek, Robert, 51

Index

Labor unions, support for training and retraining programs, 5, 42
  cooperative programs with management, 47–49, 50, 51
  team member of retraining program teams, 71–72
Long-range planning, 54–55, 148–49
  personnel plans, 56–57

Management-labor cooperative retraining programs, 47–49, 50–51
Managers
  changing skills for, 25–28
  displacement of, 2–3, 10–11
  effect of automation on, 15–17
  soliciting input from top, in linking corporate goals to retraining programs, 55–56
Manufacturing jobs, 2, 12
Medicaid, 123
Microprocessor technology, 15–16, 22–23
Motorola Corporation, 55

National Center for Education Statistics, 146
National Development and Training Center, 48
National Pilot Program, 49
National Science Foundation, 3
New jobs, skills required for, 2

Occupational retraining, 43
Offices
  automation in, 10–11, 21
  team approach in, 21
Older workers, 122–43, 152–53
  characteristics of, 128–29
  defining the category of, 125–28
  entrance of, into retraining programs, 131–33
  intellectual performance and age, 129–30
  as learners in the classroom, 133–38
  reasons for retraining, 122–25
  summary and implications of, 140–42
  transitions of, 139–40

Onan Corporation, 41
Opinion Research Corporation, 4
Organizational pyramids, corporate, 16

Packard Electric, 73
Participatory management, 18
Partnerships for retraining, 43–51
  business-education cooperation, 49–51
  government-private initiatives, 44–47
  management-labor cooperation, 47–49
Personal priorities, worker's, 101–2, 126–27
Personnel member, retraining program team, 70(table), 71
Personnel plans, 7
  long-term vs. short-term, 56–59
Placement process, after retraining programs, 81–82, 97–98
Planning, linking training to, 54–55
Planning for Partnerships program, 82
Planters Peanuts, 49
Polaroid Corporation, 41
Private Industry Councils (PICs), 44
Private sector, responsibility in retraining, 7
Production teams, 19–21
Professional development, 84, 85
Program manager, retraining program teams, 72, 150
Publicizing retraining programs, 89–92, 98, 151
  messages for employees, 91
  messages for managers, 90–91
  messages for the general public, 91–92

Quality circles, 18, 19
Quality of Worklife (QWL) program, 73

Relocation, 115, 117–18
Remedial education, 35–42
Retraining. *See also* Remedial education; Training

Index

Retraining (cont.)
  corporate commitment to, 146–48
  corporate departments involved in, 7–8
  defined, 5–6
  economic imperative for, 1–5, 144–45
  vs. firing/hiring, cost/benefit comparisons, 64–66
  implications of, 43–51
  linked to corporate goals (see Corporate goals and retraining)
  occupational, 43
  for older workers (see Older workers)
  partnerships for, 43–51
  responsibility for, 7
  vs. training, 5–6
Retraining programs, 68–89. See also Transitions, facilitating worker's
  announcing and publicizing, 89–92, 151
  developing curriculum plan, 83–89
  developing program plan, 73–83, 149–51
  entrance of older workers into, 131–33
  evaluation, 94–96
  forming retraining teams, 68–73, 150
  implementation, 92–94
  special issues in, 96
  stages in, 69(table)
  summary and implications, 97–98
Retraining program team, 68–73, 150
  responsibilities of, 70(table)–73
Retrographics Business Group (RBG), 72–73
Robotics, 2, 22, 58
Rochester Institute of Technology, 73
Roles and responsibilities, retraining program plan, 75
Rosenthal, Stephen, 19
Rosow, Jerome, 7

Saab company, 20
Saturn Corporation, 20
Selection process and criteria, for retraining program candidates, 77–81, 97, 132–33

Service jobs, 2, 12–14
  level of skills vs. nature of skills, 13–14
Skills requirements
  analysis of, in retraining program plans, 75–76
  assessing demand for, 59–61
  assessing supply of, 61–62
  basic, 30–32, 145–46
  imbalances in, 63–64
  job design and, 18–21
  for managers, 25–28
  organizational factors affecting, 11
  planning for corporate needs in, 56–59
  restructuring of the economy and, 11–14
  technical skills affecting, 22–24
  technology affecting, 17–18
Skills and knowledge analysis, assessing demand for skill requirements through, 60–61
Skills inventory/analysis, worker, 61–62, 103–4
Skills mismatch in the workplace, 1–4, 144
Smith, Robert, 3
Social interaction skills
  required in management positions, 26–27
  required in service occupations, 14
Social Security system, 123
Sociotechnical analyses, 60
Stober, Linda, 42
Strategic mission, corporate, and human resource planning, 5
Strategic planning, 54–55, 148–49
Stress and anxiety among workers, 107, 110–12, 120, 126, 136–38, 141, 152
  long-term, 112–19

Teaching methods in retraining programs, 87–88
  older learners, 133–38
Technical skills
  effect of, on skills requirements, 22–24
  needed by managers, 27–28
  shortage of, 3–4
Technological innovation
  adjusting to, 15–17

· 158 ·

Index

as a cause of displaced workers, 3
effect on nature of work, 24–25
effect on skills requirements, 17–18
role of corporate culture and, 28–30
Tests, using to evaluate trainees, 85–87
Trade Adjustment and Assistance Program, 44
Trainees in retraining programs
  agreement of, with the company, 82
  alleviating training stress, 110–12, 120, 126, 136–38, 141, 152
  assisting with long-term stress, 112–19
  deciding on selection process and criteria for, 77–81, 97, 132–33
  effect of family and friends on, 114–16
  facilitating transition of, 110–19
  older workers (*see* Older workers)
Training, 146
  overview of workplace, 34–35
  vs. retraining, 5–6
Training Magazine, 35
Transition: Making Sense of Life's Changes (Bridges), 116, 142
Transitions, facilitating worker's, 84, 99–121, 151–52
  assisting retrainees, 110–19
  easing impact of company changes on workers, 107–10
  keeping up with change through career planning, 99–107, 120
  older workers, 139–40, 142
  summary and implications of, 119–21
Travelers Insurance, 55

United Auto Workers of America, 42
  cooperative retraining and skills programs, 47–48, 49–50
U. S. Department of Education, 3
U. S. Department of Labor, 45, 49, 125
U. S. Senate Special Committe on Aging, 129

Volvo company, 20

White-collar workers, skills shifts, facing, 2–3, 10–11, 146

Worker(s)
  assessing supply of skill requirements by identifying skills of, 61–62
  career planning for, 99–107
  displaced (*see* Displaced workers)
  need for/lack of basic skills among, 4, 30–32, 52, 145–46
  older (*see* Older workers)
  in retraining programs (*see* Trainees in retraining programs)
  shortages of, 3
  stress and anxiety among, 107, 110–19, 120, 126, 136–38, 141, 152
  transition of, to changes within the company, 107–10
Worker responsibility and control, increasing, 14, 18
Workforce, future trends in, and older workers, 122–24
Work in America Institute, 64, 131
Worklife Transition (Barton), 128
Workplace, 9–33
  adjusting to technology in, 15–17
  displaced workers in, 9–11
  economic changes and, 11–14
  job design and skills requirements in, 18–21
  managerial skills in, 25–28
  role of corporate culture in, 28–30
  skills mismatch in, 1–4, 144
  summary of changes in, 30–32
  technical skills needed in, 22–24
  technology and nature of work in, 24–25
  technology and skills requirements in, 17–18
Workplace training, overview of, 34–35
  general types of, 37(table)
  general types of, by industry, 38–39(table)
  general types of, by size of organization, 40(table)
  who gets training, 36(table)
World economy, 3

Xerox Corporation, 72–73

Zemke, Ron, 51